Practical Business Studies

Purchasing

Marlies Hemmer-Hiltenkamp, Paul Kavanagh,
Margit Bentin, Jürgen Böker, Thomas Kreye,
Thomas Meyer, Klaus Richter, Siegfried Rothe

westermann

Contents

Preface

The increasing economic net in the European Union and the internationalisation of the markets demand higher communication skills in foreign languages. To cope with concrete professional demands the English language plays an increasingly important role.

This workbook is based on professional communication situations and teaches specific knowledge not only in the English language, but also in the field of economics as well and therefore aims at enabling the student to react to different business situations in a professional manner.

The subject "purchasing" is dealt with in form of a case-study from the point of view of the model company MoDo Office Service Ltd. that is situated in the south of England. Reality-true tasks regarding the purchase of an environmentally-friendly product are to be coped with. They include the process of looking for and finally finding a suitable supplier, the comparison of quotations and the placing of an order as well as its booking.

The students learn by doing, all the decisions are made by them. This decision-making is supported by the communication exercises in this book. Communication is the key word and our main aim has been to especially increase the professional communication skills of all the participating students who have to solve all the problems in group work and to find mutually acceptable solutions.

The workbook includes a one-language definition of the vocabulary, just where it is needed, i. e. on the page where the word is used first. In addition, terms and phrases often used in commercial English and correspondence are presented in a communicative context of appropriate situations to ensure a successful learning. The appendix includes a role play and some vocabulary exercises. An alphabetical vocabulary section in four languages (English, German, French and Spanish) has been included at the end of the book.

We hope that you will enjoy working with this book and improve your knowledge of the English language and economics at the same time.

Authors and editors Braunschweig, autumn 1996

Ideograms

The following ideograms help you to find your way through the book.

The process of purchasing is dealt with in chronological order. It starts on 2 May and ends on 21 June. It is continued from 16 September when offers of foreign suppliers are compared to those of British ones. Activities that are closely connected are performed on the same working day.

This ideogram shows that legal or economic information is given that is needed to do the tasks in order to solve the case.

Mathematical subjects are included in the case of purchasing. This ideogram shows that it is advisable to use the pocket calculator to solve the mathematical problems.

The PC ideogram shows when new technology can be used if regarded as helpful.

This ideogram marks the tasks you have to do. You should write down your answers in pencil so that you can correct them – if necessary – when the results are presented and discussed in class.

This ideogram shows when a discussion of your results with the help of your teacher or trainer seems to be useful. As only suggestions are made the arrangement of the evaluation phases can be varied.

The vocabulary is explained in English on the bottom of the page where the word is used first. The German, French and Spanish equivalents of the words given are to be found in the appendix.

Exercises are optional and only intend to improve your knowledge of the English language. They needn't be done in order to proceed and find the solution of the case in question.

We are the wholesale company MODO OFFICE SERVICE LTD. in West Byfleet, SURREY, and supply customers within a range of about 100 miles.

our company's premises

We sell the following lines:

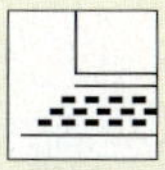 1 Office machines

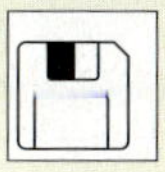 2 Computer accessories

 3 Writing implements

 4 Office paper

 5 Technical drawing equipment

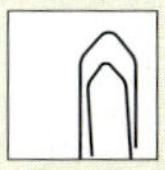 6 General stationery

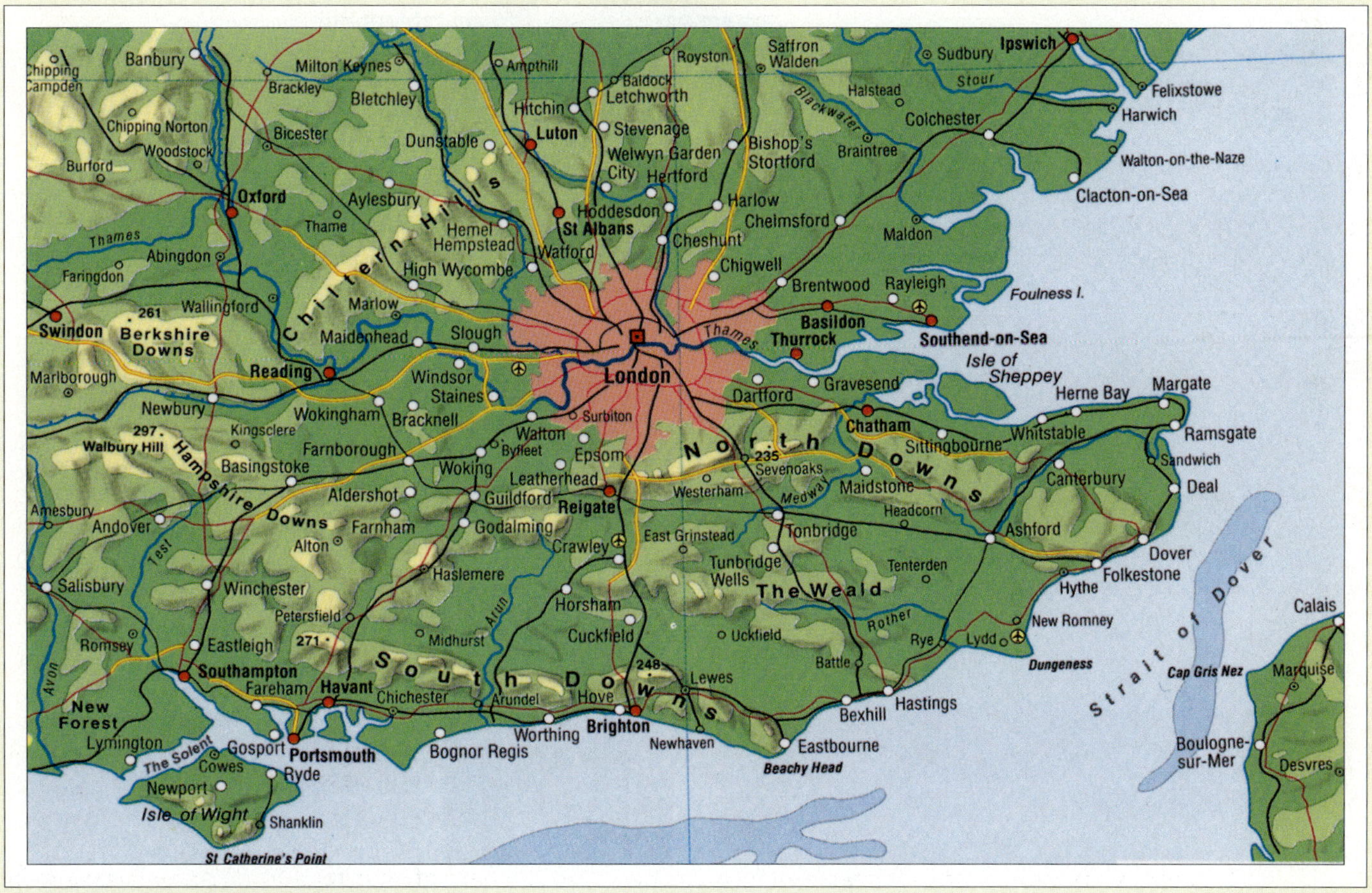

map showing the south of Great Britain

V

vocabulary

accessories	something that is added to something else	stationery	materials used in the office
equipment	things needed for a particular purpose	to supply	to provide
furniture	movable things, tables, desks	wholesale company	company selling large quantities of goods to retailers
range	the distance within which you can see or hear		

There are twenty-three persons working for our company, of which twenty are staff members and three are trainees. The head of the company, the managing director, is supported by the managers of the following departments: purchasing, sales, warehouse and administration. Our 280 customers are looked after by five travelling salesmen from our sales department.

Management
Managing Director:
Elizabeth Painter

Secretary:
Sally Wood

Purchasing Department:
Manager: Pat Green

Clerks:
Jennifer Bower
Susan Hare

Trainee:
David Stain

Sales Department:
Manager: Tom More

Employee:
James Jackson

Trainee:
Mary Hills

Representatives:
Julie King, Angela Arnold, Gavin Black, Chris Fell, Dennis Frost

Warehouse Department:
Manager: Julie King

Clerk:
Penny Arnold

Warehouse assistants:
John Smith
Marc Bentin

Administration Department:
Manager: Paul Lovecake

Accountants:
Sean Hunter, Audrey Winter

Trainee:
Samantha Steel

Caretaker:
Gordon Pane

Departments and their staff

V *vocabulary*

administration department	management of business affairs
purchasing department	department that is responsible for buying goods
representatives	sales personnel
sales department	department that is responsible for selling goods
staff member	person working for a company (employee)
trainee	person learning how to do a job
warehouse department	department concerned with the storage of goods

E

Exercises:

Have a look at the following list. Decide which of the following activities is performed by which department and discuss your results with your neighbour.

a) to place orders

b) to store goods

c) to put a caller through

d) to inform customers about special offers

e) to enter incoming invoices into the books

f) to pay salaries to the employees

g) to hire employees

h) to send enquiries to suppliers

i) to compare incoming offers

j) to present products at a fair

Task 1:

Do the following task in your group and present your results in front of the class. Prepare a company profile of MODO Office Service Ltd. with reference to the following points:

- Types of products sold
- Location of the company
- Its sales area

- Customer target group
- Type of company
- Internal structure of the company
- Size of the company
- Purpose of the company
- Position of the company in the economy as a whole

E

Exercises:

1. Those of you already working, please present your company in the same way as above.

2. Form questions referring to the key terms in Task 1.
   Ex.: What goods does MODO sell?

   a)

   b)

   c)

   d)

   e)

   f)

   g)

2 May

Mr More, our sales manager, looks at the reports received from his salesmen last week. Four of them sent in written reports, the fifth gave his report in on the telephone, as he was short of time.

Wood-free paper – recycled paper

wood-free paper:
This paper is produced from cellulose (derivative of wood) and to some extent from rags (cotton and linen).

recycled paper:
This product is made either to 100 % from waste paper or to a great extent.

from: R[1] 01 Harriet King
Reply required: <u>yes</u>/no
EDP[2] Code: 18-032 and 19-010

Information: Gp No.4 office paper

a) Bank-post paper A4, 80g., wood-free, sales down. Competitors 10% cheaper.

b) Demand changed from typewriting paper 70g. to 80g., A4, wood-free.

c) Carbon copy paper, wood-free, A4, yellow, considerable orders as competitors have increased prices by 5% - 9% in Kent.

Samples given:			Send samples to:		
Article No.:	Quantity:	To:	Article No.:	Quantity:	To:

from: R[1] 02 Jenny Arnold
Reply required: <u>yes</u>/no
EDP[2] Code: 17-010-17-033

Information: Gp No.4 office paper

1. Complaint about photocopy paper A4, wood-free: assorted colours cause blockage. Drop in sales, if the problem is not solved!
2. Offset paper A4, wood-free, white, sales stagnating
3. Demand for photocopy paper (recycled) A4, 80g., in the area N/E London; competitors can supply!

Samples given:			Send samples to:		
Article No.:	Quantity:	To:	Article No.:	Quantity:	To:

our representatives' reports

vocabulary:

assorted	various kinds	to a great extent	to a high degree
bank-post paper	special kind of paper	rags	old clothes, waste clothes, pieces of cloth
blockage	the paper gets stuck	recycled	made out of material that has been used before
carbon copy paper	paper used for making copies when typing a text	sales movement	fewer or more goods are sold
cellulose	material made from wood	to be short of something	to lack, not have something
competitor	company that offers the same product	to solve	to find an answer to a problem, to make something clear, to explain
complaint	statement of dissatisfaction	to stagnate	to stay the same
considerable	great in amount or size	wood-free	no wood is used for the production of this kind of paper
demand for	desire of customers for goods or services		
to be a derivative of/ to derive from	to come from, to be made out of something		
drop	decrease		

[1] R: representative
[2] EDP: electronic data processing

from: R: 03 Gavin Black
Reply required: yes/no
EDP Code: 39-010227 and 39-010236

Information: Gp No. 4 office paper

Typing paper A4, 80g., wood-free, not in order: watermark cannot be seen; loss in sales.
Enquiry about recycled photocopy paper A4, 80g. from 8 companies in the Guildford area.
Transparent paper A3, 100g. enquired about to a small extent in the Heathrow area; up to now not part of our range - are there any other enquiries from colleagues?

Samples given:			Send samples to:		
Article No.:	Quantity:	To:	Article No.:	Quantity:	To:

from: R: 04 Chris Fell
Reply required: yes/no
EDP Code: 12 ... and 13 ...

Information: Gp No. 4 office paper

In the central area of London repeated demands for recycled copy paper A4, 80g., and some enquiries about A3, 80g.
Can our suppliers deliver?
Photocopy paper wood-free A4, 80g.: turnover down
Typing paper A4, 70g. wood-free: turnover down
Competitors' discount for 2 million sheets and upwards much better!

Samples given:			Send samples to:		
Article No.:	Quantity:	To:	Article No.:	Quantity:	To:

our representatives' reports

E

Exercises:

Decide if the following statements are true or false.

	True	False
1. Jenny Arnold reported that white photocopy paper causes blockages.		
2. The demand for carbon paper has increased according to Mr Fell.		
3. Gavin has heard of interest in recycled photocopy paper in the Guilford area.		
4. Harriet reported that the bank paper turnover has gone down by 10 %.		
5. Mr Black wrote that the sales of typing paper A4, 80 g. have decreased.		
6. Jenny stated that the prices of A4 carbon paper have increased in Kent.		
7. Miss Arnold stated that sales of offset paper A4, wood-free have remained constant.		
8. Chris said that the turnover of wood-free paper A4, 70 g. has passed the 2 million mark.		

V

vocabulary:

colleague	fellow worker
to deliver	to provide, to supply
discount	deduction in price for goods
enquiry	request for information
loss	act of losing something
transparent	allowing light to pass through
turnover	money earned by selling goods
watermark	sign you can see in the paper when it is held against the light

MEMO

for: Mr More
from: Mr Frost
tel. no.:
fax:
[x] telephone [ ] personally
date: 29 April 19..
time: 3 p.m.

Please
[ ] offer [ ] answer [ ] confirm
[x] comment [ ] process [ ] call back
[ ] carry out [x] your info
[ ] permit [ ] check

Ref.: Report 17th week

1 (Office machines): Customers continually asking about telephone answering machines
2 (Computer accessories): Sales constant
3 (writing implements): Customers increasingly demand natural lead-pencils, considerable drop in sales of biros in 4 colours; continual high turnores in felt & fibre pens (large customer Messrs King & S. enquire about a special discount for their company's anniversary)
4 (Office paper): Two large customers in Luton enquire about a considerable amount of recycled photocopy paper A4, 80 g. Check purchase

taken/signature: P. Hills

Mr Frost's report

E

Exercises:

1. Act out the telephone call in which Mr Frost informs his company.
2. Imagine that Mr Frost did not succeed in calling someone in the company, so he sends a fax or writes a letter. Write either the fax or the body of the letter.

Task 2:

Complete the tables on the next pages using the information given by our five representatives. Do this in the following way:

a) Enter the information of each of the representatives concerning the articles of group 4 in the columns accordingly (page 12 and 13).
b) What conclusions should we obtain from the information given? Enter your results in the last line column of the first table.

V

vocabulary:

amount	quantity	felt&fibre pens	pen with a cloth tip
anniversary	birthday	implements	tools
biro	ball-point pen	increasingly	more and more
to check	to examine	to permit	to allow
to confirm	to say that something is true	telephone answering machine	machine on which the caller can leave a message
continually	without being stopped		

Table 1

Analysis of representatives' reports on articles **included** in the company's range of products **Group: 4**

Repre-senta-tive No.	Article	Turnover (increasing: + / decreasing: – / stagnating: 0)	Competitors' reaction	Customers' reaction: complaints	Customers' reaction: wishes/trends	Measures to be taken
1	bank-post paper A4, 80g., wood-free	–	price decrease	none	price reduction	– get better whole-sale price – grant higher quantity discount

V **vocabulary:**

to decrease	to make or become less
to include	to be a part of something
price reduction	lowering the price
quantity discount	a customer can pay a lower price if he buys a large quantity of the goods
range of products	all the goods sold by the company

Table 2

Analysis of representatives' reports on articles **not included** in the company's range of products **Group: 4**			
Representative No.	**Article**	**Demand in the sales area**	**Sales potential**

As usual, Mr More sends copies of the reports to Mrs Green, the head of the purchasing department. She is responsible for the purchase of all products.

Task 3:

What can you see from table No. 2 (page 13) that can influence our range of goods in the future?

In order to solve the stock problem, Mrs Green checks the suppliers who can offer this copy paper. She finds out that only suppliers 4/01 and 4/03 in the category "office paper" sell copy paper.

Suppliers — Paper Group 4 (Office Paper)

Supplier-No.	Address of the supplier	Tel. No.	Fax No.
4/01	Glade Converting Ltd. Union Mill, Valley Road ROCHDALE OL11 1TA	0706/39421	0706/860109
4/02	Hersham Papers 32 Vaux Crescent Walton-on-Thames SURREY KT12 4HD	0933/224468	0933/265567
4/03	Mayfield Ltd. Queens Road Halfway SURREY KT12 6HE	0931/288376	0931/288657
4/04	Webster Plc Paper House 1 High Street, Surbiton SURREY DS7 3TNL	0786/388376	0786/386231

Photocopy paper

Special photocopy paper, wood-free for the best quality reproductions. Can be used in all dry photocopiers and lasers. The very best quality for double sided copying. Virtually dust-free with absolute minimum of friction.

Order No.	Size	Weight	Colour	Sheets per pack
99/0020	A3	80g/m^2	Brill-white	500
99/0021	A4	80g/m^2	Brill-White	500

Laser photocopy paper – special paper only for laser printers and photocopy machines. Best print guaranteed.

99/0031	A4	80g/m^2	White	250

Xerography paper wood-free for dry photocopiers and typing. Colours available yellow, green, pink and blue.

99/0041	A4	80g/m^2	colour*	500

* please quote which colour.

Photocopy paper

Mayfield's brilliant copy paper. Universal paper of first-class quality for all dry photocopy machines (including IBM 3-4) 80g/m^2 white and coloured 500 sheets per pack. 5000 sheets per carton. A3 supplied in cartons of 2500 sheets.

Order No.		
5800	A4	white
5241	A4	yellow
5242	A4	green
5243	A4	blue
5244	A4	pink
5245	A4	beige
5801	A3	white

Mayfield's special colour* paper
Ideal for ink-jet printers and laser photocopy machines.
Specifications as above.

5015	A4
5237	A3

* please quote which colour.

extracts taken from our suppliers' catalogues

vocabulary:

to be responsible for something	legally or morally obliged to take care of something

Task 4:

What conclusions can Mrs Green draw from the excerpts of the suppliers' catalogues for any eventual addition of a new product to the company's range?

After discussing the matter with the manager, Mrs Painter, Mrs Green takes the necessary steps to include the required copy paper into the range.

Task 5:

Consider which steps we must take in order to be able to offer our customers the product in the near future.

a) Make your proposals either in writing or as a sketch.
b) Discuss with your fellow students in which order these steps must be taken.

vocabulary:

addition	extra part
conclusion	belief or opinion that is the result of reasoning
to consider	to think about something in order to come to a decision
excerpt	part of something
proposal	suggestion

Printing-Board-Wood-free

Arjo Wiggins Fine Papers Ltd.
The British Paper Company
James Cropper plc
Federal Tait Paper
Glade Converting Ltd.
Guppy Papers
James River Pine Ltd.
Mayfield Ltd.
St. Regis Hollins
Weir Paper Products Ltd.

Printing Paper Tinted

The British Paper Company
Henry Cook Ltd.
Crash & Crash Ltd.
James Cropper plc
Empire Papers
EMS Colours
Federal Taint Paper
Glade Converting Ltd.
Guppy Papers
James River Pine Ltd.
Mayfield Ltd.

Printing Paper – White

ABC Papers plc
The British Paper Company
Better Papers Ltd.
James Cropper plc
Federal Taint Paper
Glade Converting Ltd.
Guppy Papers
James River Pine Ltd.
Mayfield Ltd.
Yours only Papers Ltd.

Printed Paper Woodfree White

ABC Papers plc
The British Paper Company
James Cropper plc
Federal Taint Paper
Glade Converting Ltd.
Guppy Papers
Hersham Papers
Riverside Ltd.
Rose Co Ltd.
James River Pine Ltd.
Mayfield Ltd.
Yours only Papers Ltd.
XYZ Paper Ltd.

Recycled Copy Paper

ABC Papers
The British Paper Company
Bright Boards Ltd.
Guppy Papers
Paper Mills plc

Recycled Other Paper & Boards

The British Paper Company
Glade Converting Ltd.
Guppy Papers
Grey & Blue Boards plc
James River Pine Ltd.
Paper Mills plc

Recycled Office Paper

ABC Papers plc
The British Paper Company
Bright Co. Ltd.
Glade Converting Ltd.
Guppy Papers
Hersham Papers
Mayfield Ltd.
Major & John Ltd.
Mayfield Ltd.
Paper Mills plc
Webster plc

Recycled Tinted

The British Paper Comapny
David John Paper Mills
Glade Converting Ltd.
Guppy Papers
Hersham Papers
Mayfield Ltd.
Paper Mills plc
Sappi Mills

Recycled Uncoated Printings

ARJO Wiggins Fine Papers Ltd.
Federal Taint Papers
Glade Converting Ltd.
Guppy Papers
Hersham Papers
Paper Mills plc
Webster plc

Recycled Xerography

The British Paper Company
Better Papers
James Cropper plc
Empire Papers
Glade Converting Ltd.
Guppy Papers
Holex Papers & Tissue Ltd.
Mayfield Ltd.
Paper Mills plc

Company Addresses

Company	Location
ABC Papers Ltd.	Roach Road, Exeter, DEVON, Lancs EX1 1AA
Arjo Wiggins Fine Papers Ltd.	PO Box 88, Norwich, NORFOLK, Hants NR1 1AA
Bright Boards Ltd.	Commercial Road, Taunton SOMERSET, TA1 1AA
The British Paper Company	Apsley, Ipswich, SUFFOLK, IP1 1AA
The Brush Paper Ltd.	Commissioners Road, Strood, ROCHESTER, KENT, ME2 4ED
James Cropper plc	KENDAL, Cumbria LA9 6PZ
Empire Papers	London Road, Greenhithe KENT, DA9 9EH
Federal Tait Paper	INVERTURIE, Aberdeenshire
Glade Converting Ltd.	Union Mill, Valley Road, ROCHDALE OL11 1TA
Grey & Blue Boards, plc	Woodburn Green, HIGH WYCOMBE, Bucks, HP10 0DB
Guppy Papers	35 High Street, Surbiton SURREY, KT83 4LS
Hersham Papers	32 Vaux Crescent, Walton-on-Thames, SURREY KT12 4HD
Holex Paper & Tissue Ltd.	South Darenth, Dartford, KENT DA4 9AU
James River Pine Ltd.	ST. ANDREWS, Five KY11 1ES
Mayfield Ltd.	Queens road, Halfway SURREY KT12 6HE
Major & John Ltd.	Gloucester Road, CHELTENHAM, Glos. GL51 8NH
Paper Mills plc	12 Kings Road, Hersham, SURREY, KT12 5FH
Sappi Mills	HEMEL HEMPSTEAD, HP3 9XT
ST Regis Hollins	Newton Kyme, Tadcaster, NORTH YORKSHIRE, LS23 9SU
Webster plc	Paper House, 1 High Street, Surbiton, SURREY DS73 TNL
Weir Papers Products Ltd.	ALLOA, Scotland, FK10 4AE
Weybridge Pulp	Bridge Street, RAMSBOTTOM, BL0 0BS
Yours only Papers Ltd.	Pool in Wharfedale, Otley, WEST YORKSHIRE, LS21 1RP

Task 6:

Solve the following problem of finding a suitable supplier.

a) Describe in detail how Mrs Green went about looking for the supplier.

b) Which supplier would be most suitable with regard to the distance for delivery ? (see area map on the next page).

c) Which other sources of information could Mrs Green have used?

vocabulary:

suitable	appropriate

South-English Counties

3 May

Mrs Green decides to contact the two nearest companies and to enquire about their terms of sale (terms of payment and delivery).
She gives the task of obtaining this information to Mrs Bower.

Mrs Green and Mrs Bower

Task 7:

Write an enquiry to the two most suitable suppliers. Please use the terms and phrases given on page 23 for your letter. Enter the address in the space provided. Should you use a PC please copy the sheet at the end of this book (appendix).

Enquiry

I. The commercial and legal importance of the enquiry
The purpose of an enquiry is to obtain information. It serves to begin a commercial relationship and is without obligation.

Informal enquiry:
This is the most common form of enquiry and is used in the retail trade. A person enters a shop and asks about a certain article and its price.

General enquiry:
The request for general information and perhaps also samples. You want to know what the company can supply and its prices.

Specific enquiry:
In this form of enquiry you ask for detailed information about a specific product including samples.

II. The contents of an enquiry

1. reason for the enquiry
2. description of the goods
3. quantity
4. quality
5. price, discounts, etc.
6. kind of packing
7. time of delivery
8. terms of payment
9. terms of delivery

vocabulary:

common	ordinary, usual	sample	part of a whole to show what the rest is like
delivery	supply	supplier	person who delivers the goods
packing	material used to protect goods from damage	to supply	to deliver
request	asking for, desire	terms of payment	way how payment is effected
retail trade	shops that sell goods in small quantities	terms of delivery	way how delivery is effected

i

Business Letter

HERSHAM PAPERS

1 **32 Vaux Crescent**
Walton-on-Thames
SURREY KT12 4HD

2 Your ref Our ref

3 16 March 19–

Messrs Fell & Franklin (Builders)
12 Cottimore Avenue
4 Walton-on-Thames
SURREY
KT12 5FG

5 Dears Sirs

6 Enquiry

xxxxxxxxxxxxxxxxxxxxxxxxxxxxxxxxxxxxxxxxxxxxxxxxxx
xxxxxxxxxxxxxxxxxxxxxxxxxxxxxxxxxxxxxxxxxxxxxxxxxx
xxxxxxxxxxxxxxxxxxxxxxxxxxxxxxxxxxxxxxxxxxxxxxxxxx
7 xxxxxxxxxxxxxxxxxxxxxxxxxxxxxxxxxxxxxxxxxxxxxxxxxx
xxxxxxxxxxxxxxxxxxxxxxxxxxxxxxxxxxxxxxxxxxxxxxxxxx
xxxxxxxxxxxxxxxxxxxxxxxxxxxxxxxxxxxxxxxxxxxxxxxxxx
xxxxxxxxxxxxxxxxxxxxxxxxxxxxxxxxxxxxxxxxxxxxxxxxxx

8 Yours faithfully

9 *C. F. Green*

10 C. F. Green
Hersham Papers

11 Enc.

12 2/4

Hersham Papers
Registered Office

32 Vaux Crescent
Walton-on-Thames
SURREY KT12 4HD

Telephone: 0933 22 44 68
Fax: 0933 26 55 67

Registered in England
No. 210 27 83

E

Exercises:

1. Match the numbers 1-12 with the corresponding parts of the letter.

☐ Reference line/code	☐ Enclosures line
☐ Subject line (not always used)	☐ Letterhead
☐ Complimentary close	☐ Sender's signature
☐ Recipient's/addressee's name and address	☐ Sender's name
☐ Date of the letter	☐ Salutation
☐ Main body of the letter	☐ Copies line

2. Describe the layout of an English address.

3. Describe the differences between the German business letter and the British one.

4. Instead of writing a letter, phone MODO's suppliers to enquire about their terms of sale and their prices. Act out the conversation in class.

V

vocabulary:

complimentary close	greeting at the end of the letter	letterhead	top of the letter
enclosures	all things sent together with the letter	recipient/addressee	the person getting the letter
		reference line/code	dictation marks
		subject line	what the letter is about

Substitution Table (enquiry)

Dear	Sir(s) Madam Mr … Mrs … Ms …

<table>
<tr><td rowspan="2">We</td><td rowspan="2">refer to
have read</td><td rowspan="2">your</td><td colspan="3">circular
brochure</td><td rowspan="2">of</td><td rowspan="2">11 May.
2 June.</td></tr>
<tr><td>advertisement published</td><td>in the</td><td>Trade Review
Economist</td></tr>
</table>

<table>
<tr><td rowspan="2">from which we have</td><td rowspan="2">learnt
come to know</td><td rowspan="2">that you</td><td colspan="3">manufacture
produce</td><td rowspan="2">recycled paper.</td></tr>
<tr><td>are</td><td>manufacturers
producers</td><td>of</td></tr>
</table>

Interested As we are interested	in	your	articles products	we would be pleased	to receive	your current price list. an illustrated catalogue.

<table>
<tr><td colspan="2">We would also like to</td><td rowspan="2">know</td><td rowspan="3">your</td><td rowspan="3">earliest date of delivery.
terms of sale.
terms of delivery and payment.</td></tr>
<tr><td rowspan="2">Please</td><td>let us</td></tr>
<tr><td colspan="2">indicate</td></tr>
</table>

<table>
<tr><td rowspan="2">We</td><td>would</td><td>be grateful to receive
appreciate receiving</td><td rowspan="2">an early reply.</td></tr>
<tr><td colspan="2">look forward to receiving</td></tr>
</table>

Yours	faithfully sincerely

V *vocabulary:*

to appreciate	to welcome something	to be pleased	feeling or showing satisfaction
circular	printed letter sent to a large number of people	to receive	to get
		reply	answer
current	of the present time	terms of delivery and payment }	conditions at which something is bought or sold
to be grateful	feeling or showing thanks	terms of sale	terms of delivery and payment
illustrated	with pictures		
to indicate	to state		

By Appointment to
HM the Queen
Paper Merchants

MoDo

MoDo
Office Service Ltd
Office Papers

Rosemount Avenue
West Byfleet
SURREY KT14 6LE
Tel 0932 335577
Fax 0932 335580

Printed on Datacopy Laser Wove 90g/m^2

BS5750

MoDo Office Service Ltd
A member of the MoDo Group

Registered Office Rosemount Avenue West Byfleet
SURREY KT14 6LE Registered in England 1097405

Mrs Bower sends the enquiries to the suppliers and fills in a purchase stock card (original in the appendix).

Purchase Stock Card

SUPPLIERS:

1 No.

Name:

Address:

Telephone:

Fax:

Discount:

Terms of delivery:

Time of delivery:

Terms of payment:

2 No.

Name:

Address:

Telephone:

Fax:

Discount:

Minimum stock quantity:

Article number:

Notify quantity:

Article name:

Maximum stock:

Unit:

Supplier No.	date		order		acknow.* of order	invoice		amount		list price per unit		payment date
	enquiry	offer	date	quantity	date	No.	date	£	p	£	p	

purchase stock card

Task 8:

What purpose does the purchase stock card serve?

vocabulary:

acknowledgement of order	confirmation of an order
purchase stock card	a card giving information on the product, its suppliers and the terms of sale

* acknowledgement of order

Task 9:

Fill in the purchase stock card for the recycled paper and use all the data available so far (information on the goods and suppliers). According to the list of suppliers for group 4 on page 14, give the follow-up numbers for Paper Mills and Guppy Papers; enter these also on the purchase stock card. The recycled paper is to get the number 04-0187.

Mrs Bower also has to issue a purchase movements card for each article (original in the appendix); this is then passed on to Mrs King, the stock manager.

Purchase Movements Card

Article name:	Article No.:	Unit:

Minimum quantity:	Notify quantity:	Maximum quantity:

Supplier No.:	Supplier No.:
Name:	Name:
Address:	Address:

Notification of requirements (warehouse department and dispatch)					Order placed by the purchasing department						reminder
					date						
date	quantity in stock	quantity needed	date of delivery	signature	enquiry	offer	order	quantity ordered	supplier No.	approx. date of delivery	

purchase movements card

Purchase Movements Card (PMC)

The **purchasing department** enters onto the PMC all the important data concerning the article, supplier, etc. and passes it on to the warehouse department.

The **warehouse department** uses the card for re-ordering. This is done by filling in the card and returning it to the purchasing department.

The **purchasing department** then orders the required goods and enters the order onto the card which will then remain with this department that will see to it that the delivery date is kept.

Once the goods have arrived, the warehouse department sends the delivery note to the purchasing department. The purchasing department then returns the purchase movements card to the warehouse department that can then use it for its next order.

Thus the card "moves" from the purchasing department to the warehouse department and vice versa.

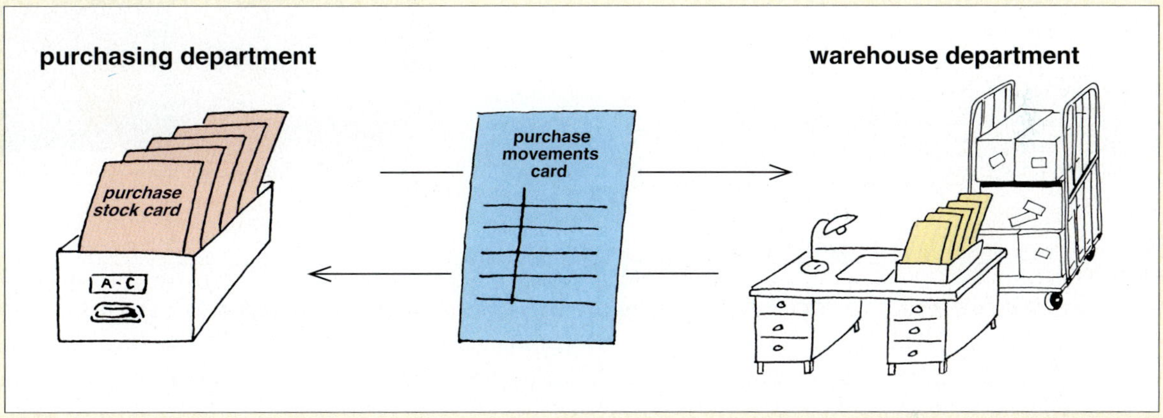

Task 10:

Enter the "recycled paper" onto the purchase movements card (see appendix); use all the data given concerning the article and its suppliers.

Write your entries in pencil.

vocabulary:

purchase movements card	with the help of this card the purchasing and the warehouse department exchange all the information needed in case of the purchase of a product
to require	to need
vice versa	the other way round

11 May

In the meantime, the new suppliers have received the enquiries.

They made offers straight away and these have now arrived in the post department where they are marked with the received stamp and date.

in the post department

Task 11:

Complete the received stamps on the offers shown on the next pages. (p. 29/p. 31)

MODO Received:

for:
- ☐ Managing Director
- ☐ Purchasing Department
- ☐ Sales Department
- ☐ Warehouse Department
- ☐ Administration Department

incoming mail stamp

The post department passes the letters on to Mrs Green, who gives them to Mrs Bower who has to check them.

Task 12:

Use the information given in the two offers to fill in the purchase stock card and the purchase movements card.

vocabulary:

marked with	to be given a sign or stamp	straight away	directly, without delay
in the meantime	meanwhile, from one definite point of time in the past until now		

GUPPY PAPERS

35 High Street
Surbiton
SURREY
KT83 4LS

MODO Received:
for:
☐ Managing Director
☐ Purchasing Department
☐ Sales Department
☐ Warehouse Department
☐ Administration Department

Surbiton, 9th May 19..

Your ref.: PG/JB Our ref.:

MODO Office Service Ltd.
Rosemount Avenue
West Byfleet
SURREY
KT14 6LE

Dear Sirs

Offer

Thank you for your enquiry. We are pleased to make the following offer:

Recycled copy paper 80 g., A4, grey packed in cartons of 5 packets @ 500 sheets			Price per 1,000 sheets
from	100,000	sheets	£ 4.45
from	500,000	sheets	£ 3.99
from	1,000,000	sheets	£ 3.73
from	2,000,000	sheets	£ 3.53

Should your order exceed the value of more than £ 2,170.00, we shall grant you a quantity discount of 10 %. For delivery with our own vehicles we charge a lump sum price of £ 25.00.

The time of delivery is 14 days after receipt of your order.

The invoice is due 4 weeks after invoice date, for payment within 14 days we grant 2 % cash discount.

The goods remain our sole property until the full payment has been received.
In all other aspects our usual general terms of sale are applicable.

Yours faithfully
p.p.

L.W. Winter
Guppy Papers

Enc.
Sample

GUPPY PAPERS Ltd.
Telephone 0932 321608
Facsimile 0932 321680

Registered Office 35 High Street Surbiton SURREY KT83 4LS
Registered in England 1026187

V *vocabulary:*

applicable	appropriate, suitable	to remain	to stay
to be due	to have to be paid	sole property	only one person owns the goods
invoice date	date given on the invoice	to the value of	to be worth
lump sum price	costs of transport		

GUPPY PAPERS

General Terms of Business

Price

1. All prices quoted in our offers are to be understood in Pounds Sterling including packing.
2. The prices are net and the valid VAT is to be added.

Terms of Delivery

1. The delivery is effected with our own vehicles, the costs are to be borne by the buyer.
2. The delivery will be effected at the risk of the buyer.

Terms of Payment

1. Invoices are to be paid within 14 days of the invoice date less 2% cash discount or within 4 weeks net.
2. For overdue payments we charge interest at the rate for overdrafts calculated by banks.
3. We reserve the right to accept cheques and bills of exchange. Cheques and bills will only be accepted at our discretion.

Right of Ownership

1. The supplied goods remain our sole property until the final sum of the invoice has been paid.
2. The buyer is obliged to inform the seller immediately, should a third person claim rights to the supplied goods.
3. The buyer is also obliged to inform the seller immediately, should the goods be confiscated by a third party.

Place of Fulfilment and Jurisdiction

Place of fulfilment and jurisdiction for both parties is Surbiton, SURREY.

Law

For the contents of the contract British law is applicable.

V

vocabulary:

bill of exchange	a document used for payment (normally within 90 days)	jurisdiction	right to exercise legal authority
to be borne	to be paid	to be obliged	to be forced
to confiscate	to take possession of something by authority	overdraft	drawing of more money from a bank account than is in it
fulfilment	bringing something to a completion	overdue	not paid at the right time
interest rate	money you pay when you borrow money from the bank	to quote	to give, to indicate
		valid	legally effective because made with the correct formalities

PAPER MILLS PLC

12 Kings Road
Hersham
SURREY
KT12 5FH
Tel.: (0932) 831578
Fax: (0932) 831590

MODO Received:
for:
☐ Managing Director
☐ Purchasing Department
☐ Sales Department
☐ Warehouse Department
☐ Administration Department

Your ref.: PG/JB Our ref.:
13 March 19..

MODO Office Service Ltd.
Rosemount Avenue
West Byfleet
SURREY
KT14 6LE

Dear Sirs

Offer

Thank you very much for your enquiry. The requested paper is in stock and we would like to submit the following offer:
Recycled copy paper, A4, 80 g.

Article	Art. No.	Price per 1000 sheets on purchase of			
		100,000	500,000	1,000,000	2,000,000
A4 grey	4001	£ 4.71	£ 4.18	£ 3.83	£ 3.60
A4 green	4002	£ 4.89	£ 4.40	£ 3.92	£ 3.72
A4 yellow	4003	£ 4.89	£ 4.40	£ 3.92	£ 3.72

We supply the paper by our own vehicles franco-domicile. For an order of the value of at least
£ 430 less 3 % discount,
£ 1.750 less 10 % discount,
£ 3.500 less 15 % discount.

Deliveries at shorter notice than 8 days are possible.

We grant you a credit of 30 days. For payment within 8 days you may deduct a 3 % cash discount.

On request we can supply other colours and shades as well as other paper sizes, as you can see from our general catalogue which is enclosed.

We hope to hear from you soon.

Yours faithfully
p.p.

A. Snowdon

A. Snowdon
Paper Mills plc

Enc.
Sample
General catalogue

PAPER MILLS PLC
Registered Office
12 Kings Road Hersham SURREY KT12 5FH
Tel.: 0932 831578
Fax: 0932 831590
Registered in England & Wales
No. 2009078

vocabulary:

to deduct	to take away from
on request	if you want
shade	indicates if a colour is light or dark

i

Offer

I. The commercial and legal meaning of the offer

An offer can be submitted orally or in writing.

Making an offer the seller expresses his intention to conclude a contract of sale provided that his offer is accepted by the buyer.

In addition to the offer most British companies enclose their general terms of business and sale which become part of the contract when they are sent to the buyer together with the offer and the seller can prove that the buyer has come to know them. Thus the companies have, for example, the possibility to exclude being made responsible for any kind of damage occuring.

Acceptance and cancellation

An offer has to be accepted within a certain time, otherwise it will expire. If there is no time mentioned the seller is supposed to be bound to it for an appropiate period of time.

An offer can be cancelled at any time unless it is accepted.

The buyer can accept the offer until it expires by being cancelled. The seller has to make sure that the cancellation reaches the customer. On the contrary, the acceptance of the offer by the buyer (order) has only to be posted to be valid and result in the conclusion of a contract of sale.

Exhibited articles

Window-displays or advertisements in newspapers and magazines are no offers; they are only exhibitions/displays addressed to the public, i.e. general information on the product or service.

II. Composition and contents of the offer

1. Reference to the enquiry (solicited offer) or presentation of the company (unsolicited offer)
2. Description of the range of products
3. Quotation of the terms of sale (prices, terms of delivery and payment, (legal) domicile, (cash) discount)
4. Polite final sentence (expressing the hope that the customer will place an order)

Task 13:

Why does Guppy Papers print its general terms of payment and delivery on the reverse side of its offers?

V

vocabulary:

to be bound to	to be obliged to do something
to expire	to come to an end
valid	being legally acceptable

i

Costs of transport

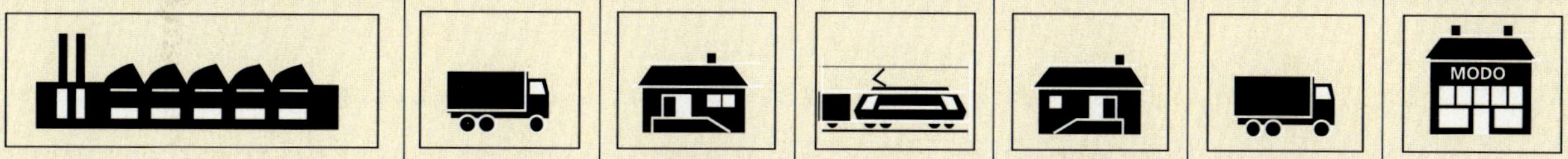

SELLER	carriage and loading	**DESPATCH STATION**	transport	**ARRIVAL STATION**	carriage and loading	**BUYER**
costs of transport / terms of delivery	cartage, i.e. local freight costs	loading costs	carriage freight	unloading costs	cartage, i.e. local freight costs	is liable for...
1. ex works ex stock	BUYER (red arrow →)					all transport costs
2. carriage forward "named address"	SELLER (blue arrow →)	BUYER (red arrow →)				transport costs ex place of despatch including loading costs
3. "free on rail" "free on board"	SELLER (blue arrow →)		BUYER (red arrow →)			transport costs ex place of despatch without loading costs
4. ex "named place" carriage paid	SELLER (blue arrow →)			BUYER (red arrow →)		transport costs from place of unloading
5. franco domicile delivered duty paid	SELLER (blue arrow →)					no transport costs at all

Red line: The buyer pays these costs
Blue line: The seller pays these costs

Task 14:

1. Define the terms of delivery in complete sentences.

2. Say which terms are the most favourable ones for the seller and the buyer.

vocabulary:

carriage forward	person receiving the goods pays for the transport
carriage paid	person sending the goods pays for the transport

Now let us get back to the offer which Guppy Papers had made. It included the following term of payment: *"the invoice is due four weeks after invoice date"*.

Task 15:

a) According to the two offers, why is the payment due after the execution of delivery?

b) In which situation would the seller require payment
- *before delivery*?
- *on delivery*?

Terms and Methods of Payment (in the home market)

Payment

before delivery	**on** delivery	**after** delivery
examples:	examples:	examples:
– pre-payment	– cash	– 3 months' credit
– 50 % deposit 50 % on delivery	– cash on delivery	– within 8 days less 3 % cash discount or 30 days net

vocabulary:

cash on delivery	the customer pays cash when the goods are handed over to him
deposit	payment in advance

In the meantime, Mrs Bower has read the offers and had a technical examination made of the samples received. Both recycled copy papers can be used on various photocopying machines without any problems. She makes a comparison of the offers to see from which supplier the paper is to be ordered. In order to do this she has to make a percentage calculation.

Commercial calculation with the aid of percentage

In order to carry out a commercial calculation a certain basic knowledge of percentage calculation must be available. To calculate discounts we use the following formula:

$$\text{Percentage value (V)} = \frac{\text{Cost (C)} \cdot \text{Percentage Rate (R)}}{100}$$

Example:

A company sells a photocopying machine at a list price of £ 1,024.00. On payment within 14 days the customer is granted a cash discount of 3 % on the list price.

Required: The amount of the percentage in £ and pence (The sum of the cash discount)

Known facts: cost = £ 1,024.00 (list price)
percentage rate = 3 (customer's cash discount)

$$\text{Percentage value} = \frac{1\,024 \cdot 3}{100} = \underline{\underline{30.72}}$$

The customer is granted a cash discount of £ 30.72.

Task 16:

Use the form on the following page to make a comparison of both offers for a minimum quantity of 100,000 sheets. Please consider quantity, quality and price. Then decide which supplier to choose.
Go to or phone a bank and ask for today's exchange rate £/DEM.

MODO OFFICE SERVICE LTD., West Byfleet, SURREY

Comparison of offers

Article No.:	Article:	Date:
Supplier: Offer of: Order quantity:		
I. Quantity comparison list purchase price less discount	£	£
= target purchase price less supplier's cash discount		
= cash purchase price + packing costs + transport costs		
= PURCHASE PRICE		
II. Quality comparison: minimum order quantity		
time of delivery		
after sales service		
further quality criteria		
order from		

Task 17:

a) What difference is there, mathematically, in the list purchase price, target purchase price, cash purchase price, purchase price?

b) Which further quality criteria should you take into consideration when comparing the offers?

c) Are the quality criteria as important as the quantity criteria?

After Mrs Bower has compared the various offers she speaks to Mrs Green. Both of them decide for Paper Mills plc in Hersham. Mrs Bower informs Mr More, the sales manager, of the price of the recycled copy paper. He then instructs one of his clerks, Mr Jackson, to work out the list price. For this he needs to know the amounts involved.

Sales calculation

Relationship between the purchase and sales calculation

The mathematical calculation of the purchase price is known as the **purchase calculation**. It is as important as the **sales calculation** which is used to work out the company's own **list sales price**.
The company has to take into account that all the costs of the company are covered and an appropriate profit can be made. In practice, the purchase price and the sales price are seen as being dependent on each other and are often worked out with reference to each other.

Steps of the **SALES CALCULATION**

HANDLING CHARGES (HC)
A percentage rate added to meet the costs of the company. The HC is added in percent to the purchase price and the result is the cost price.

PROFIT MARGIN
A percentage addition which considers the profit. It is added in percent to the cost price and the result is the cash sales price.

THE CUSTOMER'S DISCOUNT
A cash discount is a percentage reduction of the price which is expected by the customers when they pay cash. It is added in percent to the cash sales price and the result is the target sales price. The same form of calculation is used for the list sales price calculation when discount is granted.

Example: **SALES CALCULATION**

purchase price	: £ 200.00	≙ 100 %
+ **HC** 20 %	: £ 40.00	≙ 20 %
cost price	: £ 240.00	≙ 120 %
cost price	: £ 240.00	≙ 100 %
+ **profit 10** %	: £ 24.00	≙ 10 %
cash sales price	: £ 264.00	≙ 110 %
cash sales price	: £ 264.00	≙ 97 %
+ **cash discount** 3%	: £ 8.16	≙ 3 %
target sales price	: £ 272.16	≙ 100 %
target sales price	: £ 272.16	≙ 95 %
+ **discount**	: £ 14.32	≙ 5 %
list sales price	: £ 286.48	≙ 100 %

Percentage calculation for the **CUSTOMER'S CASH DISCOUNT:**

97 % ≙ £ 264.00
3 % ≙ £ X

$$X = \frac{264 \cdot 3}{97} = 8.16$$

THE CUSTOMER'S CASH DISCOUNT = £ 8.16

Percentage calculation for the **CUSTOMER'S DISCOUNT:**

95% ≙ £ 272.16
5% ≙ £ X

$$X = \frac{272.16 \cdot 5}{95} = 14.32$$

THE CUSTOMER'S DISCOUNT = £ 14.32

Task 18:

Work through the following tasks on calculations.

a) Name the types of costs which MODO must consider when adding the handling charge.

b) Why does MODO try to make a profit?

c) Why does MODO take the customer's discount into consideration in the sales calculation?

d) Which problems could occur if we were to offer our products at the price which we worked out as the target sales price?

e) Explain the commercial phrase, "profit is to be found in the purchase".

Mr Jackson works out the list sales price for the recycled copy paper. He considers the following points of calculation:

- a handling charge of 25 %
- a profit margin of 15 %
- a customer's cash discount of 2 %
- a customer's discount of 5 %

Task 19:

Work out the list sales price of 1,000 sheets recycled copy paper.
Use the purchase price and the above mentioned data.

The head of the sales department, Mr More, gives Mrs Hills, the trainee, the task to write a memo. The letter is to inform all representatives about the extended range of articles.
Mrs Hills presents her draft to Mr More who accepts and signs it.

This memo is addressed to the representatives of MODO.

By Appointment to
HM the Queen
Paper Merchants

MEMO

11 May 19..

MoDo
Office Service Ltd
Office Papers

Rosemount Avenue
West Byfleet
SURREY KT14 6LE
Tel 0932 335577
Fax 0932 335580

Dear Representatives,

Office paper: extension of the range by recycled copy paper

Due to the many enquiries received by our representatives for recycled copy paper, we have, as from now, extended our range Group 4 (office paper) to include this kind of paper.

As from 20 May we can offer our customers recyled copy paper A4, 80 g., at a list sales price of £ 6.80 per 1,000 sheets. The usual discount terms for office paper are also applicable here.

Please draw your customers' attention to this new product, pointing out that the paper is environmentally friendly, and that it can be used for all photocopying machines with no problems at all.

Yours sincerely,

Tom More

cc:

Management
Sales department
Representatives

Mrs Green asks the trainee Mr Stain to review the procedures of the purchase up to now, in preparation for his mid-term examination.

Task 20:

Please complete the following report.

Date	TASK	REASON	DEPARTMENTS INVOLVED
02 May	analyse representatives' reports	checking the representatives' reports in order to make decisions concerning the range of products	purchasing and sales departement
	look up suppliers in the trade directory		
03 May	write enquiry		
	issue purchase stock card issue purchase movements card		
11 May	compare offers		
	work out purchase price		
	work out list sales price		
	write memo		

12 May

After calculating the purchase price and the list sales price, Mrs Green asks Mrs Bower to order a small quantity of recycled copy paper first.

The Order

I. The Legal Side of the Order

The order is the acceptance of the offer by the buyer. An order without a preceeding offer is not legally binding for the seller. It can be placed both in writing or orally. In case of an oral order an immediate written confirmation is necessary in order to avoid misunderstandings.
In case of a written order the buyer only has to post it in order to conclude a contract of sale. There needn't be any proof of the seller's receipt of it. The mere posting of the order concludes the contract of sale.

An order based on an offer

A contract of sale is concluded. The company placing the order refers to the offer received. Both parties agree mutually.

An order without preceeding offer

The order must contain exact information. It is only binding for the buyer. The supplier can refuse/reject it. Only one party is bound to it, the other party can agree either through his confirmation or his delivery/supply of the goods.

Cancellation

The cancellation must be received not later than the receipt of the order, e.g. by telephone or fax. For the acceptance of the cancellation of the order, the buyer must prove that the seller has received it.

II. Composition and Contents of the Order

1. seller
2. buyer
3. reference to the offer
4. description of the goods
5. quantity
6. price
7. packing
8. despatch (form of transport)
9. terms of payment and delivery
10. date of delivery
11. marking
12. remarks
13. place of fulfilment
14. court of jurisdiction
15. inspection
16. despatch note
17. amicable arbitration
18. date
19. signatures of both parties

Task 21:

Write the order for 100,000 sheets of recycled copy paper. Use the blank letter sheet on page 46. For the body of the order refer to the substitution table on page 45.

vocabulary:

amicable arbitration	industrial referee's decision
court of jurisdiction	the place where the referee works
despatch	the sending of goods
despatch note	advice note (it tells the buyer when the goods will arrive)
place of fulfilment	the place where the goods change hands

E

Exercises:

1. The following points should be considered when placing an order. Complete the sentences below using the following words:
abroad, avoid, buyer, carefully, codes, date, invoice, marked, numbered, packing, seller, sizes, terms, unit.

1. Name the . . . . with full name and address.
2. Name the . . . . with full name and address.
3. Describe the goods very . . . . To . . . . trouble there should be no doubt about the goods ordered.
4. Quote order numbers and recognized standard . . . .
5. Always quote . . . . prices and total prices. Is the . . . . to be in £ sterling or Egyptian £? Make sure this point is clear.
6. Mention the form of . . . ., i.e. cardboard boxes, containers, paper sacks, etc.
7. Are the goods to be sent . . . . ? Then which Incoterm is applicable, FCR, CIF, FOB etc.?
8. Here you should mention the . . . . of payment.
9. When does the buyer get the goods? Make sure that the . . . . is clear.
10. At this point you must see to it that the goods are . . . . correctly.

    Are the cases to be . . . . ? Are any . . . . to be used? How is the address to be written?

2. Translate the following sentences. (Use a separate sheet.)

1. Das Angebot muss über folgende Punkte unterrichten:
2. Die Ware muss eindeutig beschrieben sein. Daher werden oft Proben, Muster, Abbildungen oder Zeichnungen beigegeben.
3. Kann nur eine bestimmte Mindest- oder Höchstmenge geliefert werden, so ist dies zu erwähnen.
4. Der Preis ist anzugeben. Dabei ist auch wichtig: mit oder ohne Verpackung oder Versandspesen, mit oder ohne Rabatt, Mengennachlass, ab Lager, frei Haus usw.
5. Die Lieferzeit und die übrigen Lieferbedingungen sind wichtig.
6. Die Zahlungsbedingungen sind bedeutungsvoll, ebenso wie der Erfüllungsort und der Gerichtsstand.
7. Soll das Angebot für eine bestimmte Zeit gelten, so ist dies anzugeben (z. B. Das Angebot ist bis zum … gültig).
8. Unter Umständen ist auf die Unverbindlichkeit des Angebots hinzuweisen (freibleibend, solange der Vorrat reicht).

V

vocabulary:

approx. = approximately	fairly correct or accurate	ex warehouse	same as ex works but from the seller's warehouse
to attach	to join something to something	invoice	bill
to enclose	to put something into an envelope	receipt	act of getting something
ex works	the buyer has to pay for all the costs for transport and insurance from the seller's premises	to refer to	to mention or speak of someone or something
		sample	specimen

Salutation (see page 23)

<table>
<tr><td>We</td><td>thank you for
have received
refer to</td><td>your</td><td>letter
offer</td><td>dated
of</td><td>12 June.
13 July.</td></tr>
</table>

<table>
<tr><td rowspan="3">Please</td><td colspan="7">enter the following order for immediate delivery.</td></tr>
<tr><td rowspan="2">send
supply
deliver</td><td rowspan="2">the</td><td rowspan="2">undermentioned
following</td><td rowspan="2">products
articles
items</td><td colspan="3">and charge them to our account.</td></tr>
<tr><td>on the</td><td>terms
condiditons</td><td>stated below.</td></tr>
</table>

Please quote the products, the quantities and prices

<table>
<tr><td rowspan="4">The</td><td rowspan="4">prices</td><td rowspan="4">given
quoted
stated</td><td rowspan="4">are</td><td colspan="2">ex works/ex warehouse.
free domicile.</td><td rowspan="4">including packing.
packing included.</td></tr>
<tr><td colspan="2">less 3% cash/quantity discount.</td></tr>
<tr><td colspan="2">in three months net.</td></tr>
<tr><td>strictly net
net cash</td><td>against presentation of documents.
one month after delivery.
at the end of the month.</td></tr>
</table>

<table>
<tr><td rowspan="2">Insurance</td><td rowspan="2">will</td><td>be</td><td>covered
obtained
effected</td><td>by</td><td>us.
you.</td></tr>
<tr><td colspan="2">cover</td><td colspan="2">all risks.
the invoice value plus 5%.</td></tr>
</table>

<table>
<tr><td rowspan="5">Payment</td><td rowspan="5">has to
should</td><td rowspan="5">be</td><td rowspan="5">made
arranged
effected
executed</td><td colspan="3">cash.</td></tr>
<tr><td>15 days
one month</td><td>after date of</td><td>shipment.
invoice.</td></tr>
<tr><td colspan="3">within 30 days after receipt of invoice.
within 3 days net.
by cheque.</td></tr>
<tr><td>documents against</td><td colspan="2">sight draft.
acceptance at 30 days' sight.</td></tr>
<tr><td colspan="3">as quickly as possible.</td></tr>
</table>

<table>
<tr><td>Delivery
Despatch
Shipment</td><td>should</td><td>be</td><td>made
arranged
effected
carried out</td><td>in August.
immediately after receipt of order.
in approx. 4 weeks.
within 15 days.</td></tr>
</table>

<table>
<tr><td rowspan="2">We</td><td rowspan="2">are relying on you
hope
trust</td><td rowspan="2">that</td><td rowspan="2">you will</td><td>give this order your</td><td>prompt
careful</td><td>attention.</td></tr>
<tr><td>execute this order</td><td colspan="2">promptly.
to our complete satisfaction.
in accordance with our instructions.</td></tr>
</table>

<table>
<tr><td rowspan="2">We look forward to</td><td>receiving an</td><td>acknowledgement of this order</td><td rowspan="2">in the near future.
soon.
by return.</td></tr>
<tr><td colspan="2">hearing from you</td></tr>
</table>

Complimentary close (see page 23)

By Appointment to
HM the Queen
Paper Merchants

MoDo

MoDo
Office Service Ltd
Office Papers

Rosemount Avenue
West Byfleet
SURREY KT14 6LE
Tel 0932 335577
Fax 0932 335580

Printed on Datacopy Laser Wove 90g/m^2

Lloyd's Register Quality Company ISO9002 BS5750

MoDo Office Service Ltd
A member of the MoDo Group

Registered Office Rosemount Avenue West Byfleet
SURREY KT14 6LE Registered in England 1097405

SALES CONTRACT

I. THE LEGAL SIDE OF A CONTRACT

- A sales contract is a bi- or multilateral agreement with legal status.
- The mutual agreement of the parties to a contract are called *OFFER* and *ORDER*.
- Under a contract both parties seller and buyer have rights and liabilities. The rights of one party are often the liabilities of the other, for example:

Punctual delivery
seller: It is his liability to deliver punctually.
buyer: He has the right to demand a punctual delivery.

Punctual payment
seller: He has the right to demand a punctual payment.
buyer: It is his liability to pay punctually.

The **conclusion of a contract** can be done in more than one way.

1. The seller makes a firm offer and the buyer accepts it unconditionally.
2. The buyer sends an order to the seller and the seller confirms it.
3. The seller sends unordered goods to the buyer and the buyer pays for them if he likes them.

The contract can be concluded verbally or in writing. It is general practice to make contracts in writing in order to avoid disputes between the two parties.

II. THE LIABILITIES OF THE TRANSACTION

a) The creation of a contract

First possibility:

SELLER —OFFER→ **SALES CONTRACT** ←ORDER (CONTRACT)— BUYER

Second possibility:

BUYER —ORDER→ **SALES CONTRACT** ←ACCEPTANCE OF ORDER (CONFIRMATION OF ORDER)— SELLER

A contract is concluded when both parties come to a mutual agreement.

b) The liabilities of the seller and the buyer

LIABILITIES

of the **seller**
- to supply the goods at the right time and place and in the right form/manner
- to transfer the rights of the goods*
- to accept the purchase price

of the **buyer**
- to accept and check the goods supplied
- to pay the agreed price at the time stipulated

* If the company's general terms of business do not include a clause referring to the ownership of the goods the property is automatically transferred on the conclusion of the contract.

see next page

vocabulary:

breach	the breaking of or failure to do what is required by an agreement, etc.
cancellation	saying that something already arranged will not take place
to stipulate	to state something clearly and firmly as a requirement

III. PERFORMANCE OF A CONTRACT OF SALE
The contract is seen to have been fulfilled when the parties to the contract have met their liabilities. Should the liabilities not have been met by one of the parties we speak of a breach of contract.

IV. CANCELLATION
The supplier should receive the cancellation at the same time or before he receives the order, e.g. as telephone message or fax.

Task 22:

Check if our order has resulted in a sales contract and if so, explain why.

Mrs Bower sends the order straight away and writes down the corresponding data on the purchase stock card and the purchase movements card.

Task 23:

Enter the order with date and quantity on the purchase stock card and the purchase movements card.

Mrs Bower files the purchase stock card and passes the purchase movements card to the warehouse. As the goods have not been in stock before, Mrs King, the warehouse manager, issues a **warehouse stock card** for the recycled copy paper (see original in appendix).

Warehouse Stock Card

Article No.:	Article name:	Unit:
Minimum stock:	Order stock:	Maximum stock:

Stock movement					Restock order		
date	document No.	receipt	exit	in stock	date	order quantity	signature

warehouse stock card

Task 24:

What is the purpose of the warehouse stock card?

Task 25:

Please complete the warehouse stock card in the appendix. Enter all relevant data for the recycled copy paper. Make your entries in pencil.

20 May

The recycled copy paper arrives at the warehouse. In the consignment is a consignment note in triplicate. Mr Smith who is responsible for incoming goods compares the contents of the consignment with the consignment note. He notes this fact on the consignment note, normally by using a rubber stamp with the wording 'Goods received and checked, date, signature'. The original (first) copy is sent to the purchasing department, the second copy is given to the driver who brought the goods (forwarding agent) as a receipt for the goods and the third copy is kept in the warehouse.

Task 26:

Compare the consignment note (page 50) with your order (page 46). Have you received the right goods?

After comparing the consignment note with the order Mr Smith makes the necessary entries in the warehouse stock card.

PAPER MILLS PLC

12 Kings Road
Hersham

SURREY
KT12 5FH

Tel.: 0932 831578
Fax: 0932 831590

MoDo Office Service Ltd
Rosemount Avenue
West Byfleet
SURREY KT12 6LE

Consignment Note - Customer Copy

Date of Despatch	Customer No.	Our Order No.	Date of Order	Document No.
20 May 19..	19230	3710	12 May 19..	2 442 052

Quantity	Unit	Description	Weight
100	@ 1,000	Recycled copy paper -grey- A4 Article No. 4001	280 kg

Total weight	280 kg
Add 5% for packaging	14 kg

Received the above in good condition

Signature

Name

goods received and checked:
Smith
Date
Signature
Date 20 May
Smith

All goods supplied to the Company's conditions of sale

consignment note

Task 27:

Complete the warehouse stock card.

Mrs Green, head of the purchasing department, receives the purchase movements card and is asked to enter the minimum, order and maximum quantities for the recycled copy paper.
She calculates the figures using a simple formula.

Purchase Movements Card

Article name:	Article No.:	Unit:
Minimum quantity:	Notify quantity:	Maximum quantity:

Supplier No.:	Supplier No.:
Name:	Name:
Address:	Address:

Notification of requirements (warehouse department and dispatch)					Order placed by the purchasing department						reminder
					date						
date	quantity in stock	quantity needed	date of delivery	signature	enquiry	offer	order	quantity ordered	supplier No.	approx. date of delivery	

purchase movements card

Stock quantities

Minimum stock

This figure represents a quantity which can only be used in case of very special delivery difficulties (e.g. strikes, lock-outs or an act of God). One also has to take into account how long a situation is likely to last before the stock can be replenished. This is normally estimated.

Order stock

When the stock has reached this level the purchasing department must be notified so that they can place a new order.

Order stock = (daily turnover x time of delivery) + minimum stock

Maximum stock:

This is the largest quantity of goods which can be stored at any one time (depending on storage capacity, perishability of the goods, etc.).

Mrs Green begins by working out the minimum stock quantity. For this, she needs to know what supply problems are likely to arise. Our general manager, Mrs Painter, has many years of experience and is therefore able to determine this quantity at a rate of demand of four days.

Mrs Green gets into touch with the head of the sales department, Mr More, to find out how the sales of recycled copy paper have developed so far.

vocabulary:

to notify	to inform somebody of something
perishable	likely to go bad quickly
to replenish	to fill something again
replenishment	action of filling something again

Mr More:	Hello!
Mrs Green:	May I speak to Tom More?
Mr More:	Speaking. What may I do for you?
Mrs Green:	I'm just doing the stock figures for our new product recycled copy paper. Remember, we told our representatives, I think it was on 11 May, that we are now taking orders for this new product.
Mr More:	Yes, I remember, wasn't it that new style ecological paper?
Mrs Green:	That's it. Well, could you let me know what orders have been received so far?
Mr More:	Hang on a moment, dear. Ah, yes, here we are, well, last week on Friday, 13 May, the first order came in for 10,000. Then this week, on Thursday, 17 May, 20,000 sheets, on 18 it was 5,000 and today 25,000, and don't forget, today is not finished yet. We may be getting some more, but I doubt it.
Mrs Green:	Ok! I've got the figures. What do we reckon the further demand is going to be like?
Mr More:	Well, if you ask me, I think it will sell quite well. In the first five days we have already sold 50,000 sheets. I reckon our weekly turnover should be about 70,000 to 90,000 sheets.
Mrs Green:	Not bad for a start. We'll keep an eye on it and see how it develops. Thank you for your help, Mr More. See you on Monday. Have a nice weekend, bye.
Mr More:	Same to you, my dear, bye for now.

During the telephone call Mrs Green has taken the following notes:

Week 19: Sheets

Fri 13 May 10,000 → 10,000 sheets

Week 20:

Tues 17 May 20,000
Wed 18 May 5,000
Fri 20 May 25,000 } 50,000 sheets

Total: 60,000 Sheets

Mrs Green has now all the necessary information to work out the minimum stock of recycled copy paper.

Task 28:

Work out the minimum stock quantity for the recycled copy paper using the following formula:

$$\text{average daily turnover} = \frac{\text{turnover per working week*}}{\text{number of working days per week*}}$$

minimum stock of recycled copy paper ≙ turnover for ________ working days

average daily turnover of recycled copy paper = ______________________ =

minimum stock reserve =

Task 29:

The heads of the company are of different opinions regarding the fixing of a minimum stock reserve.
Explain in your own words the pros and cons of a minimum and a maximum stock reserve.

vocabulary:

average daily turnover	goods sold in one day
minimum stock quantity	the lowest amount of goods to be kept in reserve

* we have a five-day-week (Monday - Friday)

Mrs Green begins to work out the quantity to be ordered.

Task 30:

a) What information is necessary to work out the order quantity?

b) Work out the order quantity using these data.

Order quantity =

Finally, Mrs Green works out the maximum stock quantity. The warehouse manager, Mr King, informs her that the storage area has a maximum capacity of 15 pallets.
Mrs Green knows that one pallet holds 40 cartons and each carton holds 2,500 sheets of paper A4.

Standard packing units in the paper industry

1 packet

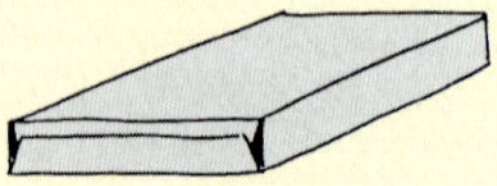

500 sheets

1 carton = 5 packets

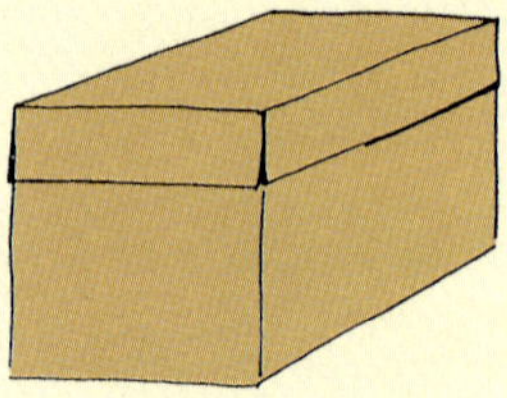

2,500 sheets

1 pallet = 40 cartons

100,000 sheets

Task 31:

How many sheets can be stored, according to the given data?

Maximum stock:

Mrs Bower, employee in the purchasing department, is then asked to work out the stock quantities and to enter these figures on the purchase movements card which is then returned to the warehouse.

vocabulary:

maximum stock quantity	the highest amount in reserve

Task 32:

Enter the corresponding values (figures) on the purchase stock card and the purchase movements card.

Mrs Bower returns the filled-in purchase movements card to Mrs King, the warehouse manager.

Task 33:

Enter the appropriate figures on the warehouse stock card.

26 May

The invoice for the goods delivered on 20 May has arrived today. The invoice is stamped and sent to the purchasing department. Mrs Bower now checks the invoice.

PAPER MILLS PLC

12 Kings Road
Hersham
SURREY
KT12 5EH
Tel.: 0932 831578
Fax: 0932 831590

MoDo Received
for:
- [ ] Managing Director
- [x] Purchasing Department
- [ ] Sales Department
- [ ] Warehouse Department
- [ ] Administration Department

MoDo Office Service Ltd
Rosemount Avenue
West Byfleet
SURREY KT12 6LE

Sales invoice

Customer's order number	Our Order No.	Supplying Sales Office	Customer No.	Invoice Date	Invoice No.	Page
	3710	Hersham	19230	20 May 19..	178-006-9	1

Quantity	Description	Size	Subs	Weight/Unit	Price £/Unit	Qty. Disc %	Value
100	Recycled copy paper -grey-	A4		2.8 kg	4.71	3	456.87

VAT % Rate	Goods Value	VAT Value
17.5	456.87	79.95

TERMS NET 30 DAYS

Goods Total £ 456.87
VAT Total £ 79.95
Invoice Total £ 536.82

invoice received from Paper Mills plc

Task 34:

Enter the invoice dates on the purchase stock card.

Checking the invoice

Providing the goods have been received in perfect condition, we now check the invoice to see if the supplier offers a cash discount for prompt payment.

Checking the contents of the invoice:

Check the type, the quality and quantity of the goods ordered. Make sure the order, consignment note and invoice match up with each other.

Checking the calculation of the price:

Look at:
- the list price
- the discount
- the total price
- the transport costs/delivery charge

Task 35:

Explain why you have to check if the contents of the invoice as well as the calculation of the price are correct.

Mrs Bower notes that the terms of payment allow for a cash discount.

Task 36:

Check whether it would be worthwhile taking advantage of the cash discount offered by paying the invoice amount immediately as the company would then have to take out an overdraft (current interest rate: 12% p.a.).

a) Work out the amount which has to be paid.

vocabulary:

overdraft	sum of money lent somebody by a bank allowing him to spend more money than is in his account
to be worthwhile	to be of any use, justify the time, money or effort that is spent

b) For how many days must we extend the overdraft with our company's bank? Check the terms of payment of the offer carefully. Allow on average three days for transferring a payment from one account to another.
Give reasons for your decision.

c) Work out the interest which will be charged by our company's bank. But, before you begin, have a look and see how the calculation is carried out.

$$\textbf{In}\text{terest} = \frac{\textbf{C}\text{apital} \cdot \textbf{P}\text{ercentage Rate} \cdot \textbf{T}\text{ime}}{100 \cdot 360}$$

$$\textbf{IN} = \frac{\quad \cdot \quad \cdot \quad}{100 \cdot 360}$$

The interest amounts to £ __________ .

Calculation of Interest

The calculation of interest is an extension of the calculation of percentages (compare page 35) by a further factor TIME.
When calculating interest, you start with three factors in order to find out the fourth.

Details of percentage calculation:

$$\text{Percentage Value (V)} = \frac{\text{Cost (C)} \cdot \text{Percentage Rate (R)}}{100}$$

Percentage Value (V)

Percentage Rate (R)

Cost (C)

$$V = \frac{C \cdot R}{100}$$

Details of interest calculation:

Capital (CPT)

Interest Rate (INR)

Interest (IN)

Time (T)

$$IN = \frac{CPT \cdot INR \cdot T}{100 \cdot 360}$$

(Formula for the calculation of daily interest)

vocabulary:

to pay interest	to pay money to the bank because of overdrawing one's account
percentage rate	part of one hundred (%)
percentage value	sum which is the result of the calculation
to take out an overdraft	to borrow money from a bank by taking more money from an account than is in it
to transfer money	to move money from one account to another

d) Taking into account the facts you have obtained so far, decide whether it would be worth using the cash discount.

e) What economical factors are of importance when making the decision whether to make use of a cash discount or not?

Having carefully checked the invoice in every detail, Mrs Bower stamps and signs it. With regard to using the cash discount she also makes a note of the deadline for payment (30 May). Then she passes the invoice on to the administration department. Mr Hunter is one of the staff members responsible for incoming invoices.

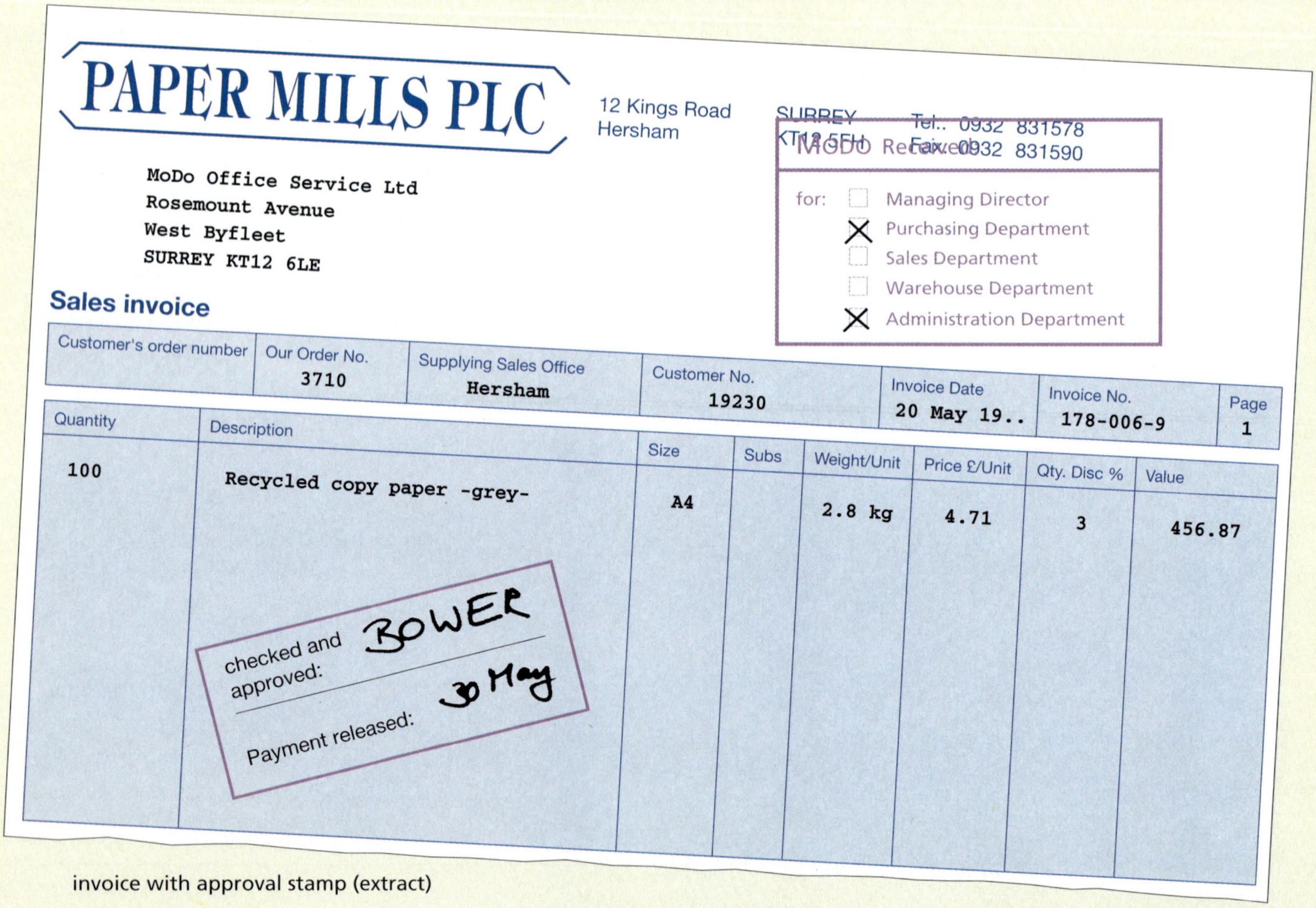
PAPER MILLS PLC

12 Kings Road
Hersham
SURREY
KT12 5FH
Tel.: 0932 831578
Fax: 0932 831590

MoDo Office Service Ltd
Rosemount Avenue
West Byfleet
SURREY KT12 6LE

MODO Received
for:
- [ ] Managing Director
- [x] Purchasing Department
- [ ] Sales Department
- [ ] Warehouse Department
- [x] Administration Department

Sales invoice

Customer's order number	Our Order No.	Supplying Sales Office	Customer No.	Invoice Date	Invoice No.	Page
	3710	Hersham	19230	20 May 19..	178-006-9	1

Quantity	Description	Size	Subs	Weight/Unit	Price £/Unit	Qty. Disc %	Value
100	Recycled copy paper -grey-	A4		2.8 kg	4.71	3	456.87

checked and approved: BOWER
Payment released: 30 May

invoice with approval stamp (extract)

V

vocabulary:

to check	to control, to inspect, to examine
to approve	to confirm, to agree
approval stamp	stamp showing that the document is correct

30
May

Mr Hunter instructs one of the trainees, Mrs Steel, to fill in a cheque in order to settle the invoice of 25 May. He also explains to her how important it is to pay debts punctually.

i

Debts and their settlement

The buyer's most important obligation is to pay the invoiced amount when it becomes due. If no particular time is stipulated the invoice is payable immediately. Although this is generally applicable, it would be difficult to sue the buyer for non-payment if the goods had not actually been delivered or the services rendered. According to the Sale of Goods Act (SofGA*) business is effected under concurrent conditions (mutual agreement), i.e. the seller must be able and prepared to transfer the product to the buyer and the latter must be able and willing to pay for it.

In the case of the **payment** of debts the **buyer** is **responsible** and must bear the costs for the payment of the **amount due**, but not only these facts are of importance, the payment of the money itself is also his responsibility. The buyer must make sure that the **due sum is received** and credited to the account of the seller, that is when the place of fulfilment is the address of the seller (usually stipulated in the contract of sale by the business partners). Should the sales contract not mention any place of payment, then the sum has to be paid at the seller's address. This is also applicable when the buyer is from abroad and has even bought in a foreign currency (not pound sterling).

It is up to the business partners themselves to decide what sum is to be paid, in which form and when the payment is to be effected.

Payment by cheque

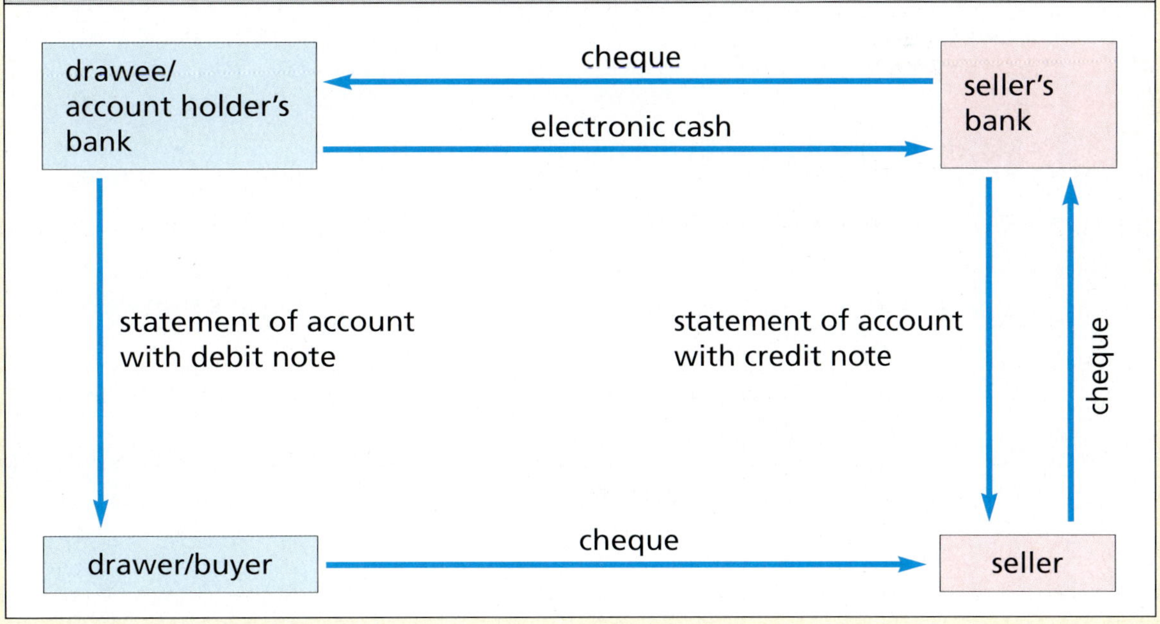

* SofGA: an act (law) for business relationships

V

vocabulary:

concurrent	mutual, agreed	latter	last mentioned
drawee	person/bank who has to pay	to render	to do
		to stipulate	to quote, mention
drawer/account holder	buyer	to sue	to take to court

Task 37:

Fill in the cheque so that Mr Hunter can check it.

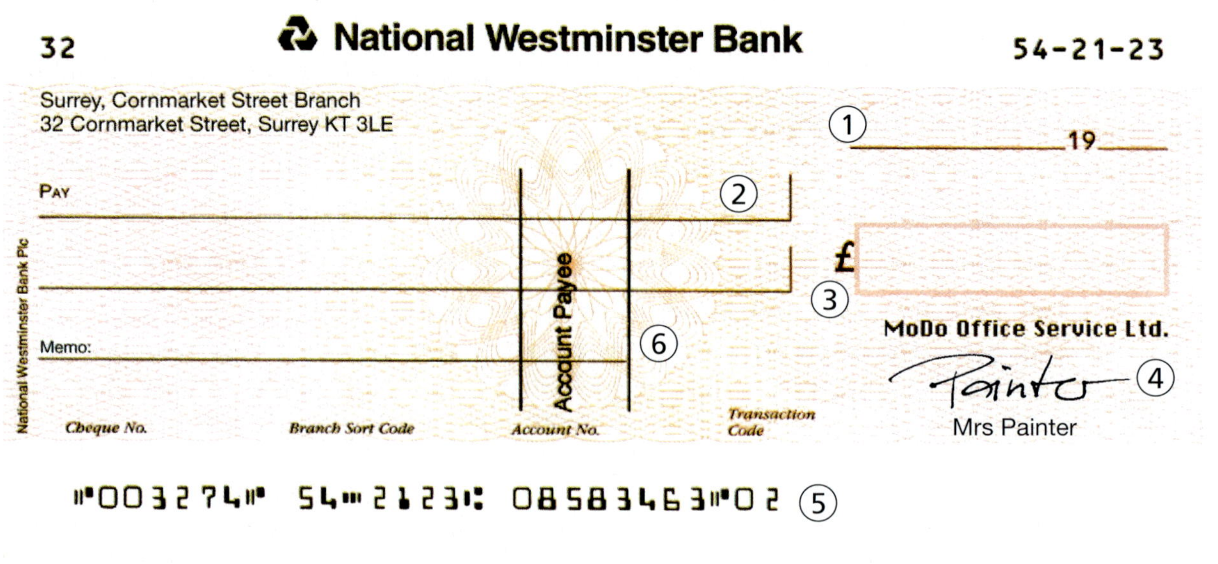
32 National Westminster Bank 54-21-23

Surrey, Cornmarket Street Branch
32 Cornmarket Street, Surrey KT 3LE

① 19

PAY ②

£ ③

Memo: ⑥

Account Payee

MoDo Office Service Ltd.

Painter ④
Mrs Painter

National Westminster Bank Plc

Cheque No. Branch Sort Code Account No. Transaction Code

⑈003274⑈ 54⑉2123⑆ 08583463⑈02 ⑤

cheque (crossed)

Mrs Steel gives the filled-in papers to Mr Hunter. He checks them and passes them on to Mrs Painter for signature. He receives them back shortly afterwards and then sends them on to the bank. At the same time he requests the purchasing department to note the payment on the purchase stock card.

Exercises:

Match the numbers with the parts of the cheque.

- ☐ reason for the payment
- ☐ payee
- ☐ cheque number, bank code, account number
- ☐ date
- ☐ payer's signature
- ☐ amount to be paid

Task 38:

Make the entries on the purchase stock card.

vocabulary:

to request	to ask

31 May

Mrs King, on making her rounds through the warehouse, realises that the stock of recycled copy paper is exhausted. She takes a look at the warehouse stock card from which she can see the turnover of the recycled copy paper.

Task 39:

Complete the following orders:

a) Enter the following data on the warehouse stock card and work out how much stock remains.

date of delivery	consignment note No.	quantity delivered
23 May	7912	10,000 sheets
23 May	7913	20,000 sheets
23 May	7914	5,000 sheets
23 May	7915	25,000 sheets
25 May	8025	10,000 sheets
27 May	8190	30,000 sheets

b) When, in your opinion, should Mrs King have drawn the attention of the purchasing department to the fact that stocks were running short?

After checking the facts with Mrs Green, Mrs King orders a further 500,000 sheets of recycled copy paper using the purchase movements card as a guide. The higher turnover so far justifies ordering this quantity.

Task 40:

Bring the purchase movements card and the warehouse stock card up to date.

Mrs King sends the purchase movements card to the purchasing department, where the order is sent to the appropriate supplier.

Task 41:

Execute the following points to complete the order:

a) Order 500,000 sheets recycled copy paper from Paper Mills plc.

b) Note the data on the purchase movements card and the purchase stock card.

The purchase movements card will then be returned to the warehouse.

vocabulary:

to be exhausted	nearly used up

By Appointment to
HM the Queen
Paper Merchants

MoDo

MoDo
Office Service Ltd
Office Papers

Rosemount Avenue
West Byfleet
SURREY KT14 6LE
Tel 0932 335577
Fax 0932 335580

Printed on Datacopy Laser Wove 90g/m^2

Lloyd's Register Quality Assurance
ISO9002
BS5750

MoDo Office Service Ltd
A member of the MoDo Group

Registered Office Rosemount Avenue West Byfleet
SURREY KT14 6LE Registered in England 1097405

1 June

In today's post is the following statement of account, which is passed on to the administration department.

National Westminster Bank — Confidential

SHEET NUMBER 16

32 CORNMARKET STREET
West Byfleet
SURREY KT 3LE

ACCOUNT
MoDo
Office Service Ltd
Rosemount Avenue
West Byfleet

ACCOUNT NO. 08583463

TELEPHONE 722621

STATEMENT DATE 31 May 19..

DATE	DETAILS	WITHDRAWALS	DEPOSITS	BALANCE (£)
				- 12,123.80
29 May	BALANCE FROM SHEET NO. 15		870.00	- 11,253.80
30 May	TR Mayfield Ltd. Goods returned			
31 May	CC Paper Mills plc Invoice 178-006-9	536.82		- 11,790.62
31 May	BALANCE TO SHEET NO. 17			- 11,790.62

National Westminster Bank Plc

Key: SO Standing Order; EC Eurocheques; DV Dividend; TR Transfer; CC Cash &/or Cheques; CP Card Purchase; Auto Withdrawals: AC Automated Cash, DD Direct Debit; PY Payroll; OD Overdrawn; Interest - see over

THE REVERSE SIDE OF YOUR STATEMENT PROVIDES DETAILS OF YOUR PERSONAL CURRENT ACCOUNT FEES.

statement of account

Task 42:

Check the statement of account to see whether the outstanding amount invoiced by Paper Mills plc has been paid on time.

Task 43:

Explain why the credit note of 30 May for £ 870.00 came about.

vocabulary:

statement of account	form stating the amount of money paid from, transferred to or withdrawn from the account

9 June

The ordered recycled copy paper from Paper Mills plc has in the meantime been delivered by one of their own lorries. On receipt of the goods no damage can be seen from the outside. Mr Smith signs and stamps the consignment note accordingly.
He gives one copy to the driver as a receipt for the goods. The other copy is given to Mrs King. The original is passed on to the purchasing department. Before the goods are finally stored in the warehouse, Mrs King has random checks made of the quality of the goods by opening some of the packages.

PAPER MILLS PLC

12 Kings Road
Hersham
SURREY
KT12 5FH
Tel.: 0932 831578
Fax: 0932 831590

MoDo Office Service Ltd
Rosemount Avenue
West Byfleet
SURREY KT12 6LE

Consignment Note - Customer Copy

Date of Despatch	Customer No.	Our Order No.	Date of Order	Document No.
7 June	19230	3921	31 May 19..	2 448 713

Quantity	Unit	Description	Weight
500	@ 1,000	Recycled copy paper -grey- A4 Article No. 4001	1,400 kg

goods received and checked: Smith
Date 9 June
Signature Smith

consignment note sent by Paper Mills plc (extract)

Rights and obligations of the partners to the contract

When two parties conclude a contract, both the seller and the buyer have rights and liabilities. Whatever the circumstances may be (non-delivery, delay in delivery or delivery of faulty goods) the buyer is entitled to claim compensation even if the seller is not responsible for the damage. Depending on the contract the buyer can either claim compensation for the loss in value of the goods or, if the breach of the contract is particulary serious, the buyer has the right to refuse acceptance of the consignment and/or return it to the seller. Which regulation should apply will be set out in the contract.

In the first case the buyer accepts and keeps the goods but he can hold the seller responsible for any damage and consequences resulting from it for a period of up to six years.

In the second case (non-acceptance) the buyer has to make his claim immediately on receipt of the goods by exercising his right to refuse acceptance of the goods and returning them to the seller. Should the buyer accept the goods knowing them to be damaged, he loses the right to return them but is still entitled to claim compensation for a period of up to six years.

Task 44:

Sum up the buyer's rights in case of the delivery of defective goods.

During the random check Mr Smith discovers that some of the cartons have got water stains on them. On a closer inspection he sees that six cartons in all had been damaged, probably rain water had penetrated the outer casing. The contents of all six packets is no longer usable. Mrs King notes the damage on a complaints sheet and passes it on to the purchasing department.

Task 45

Complete the complaints sheet.

COMPLAINTS SHEET

Supplier:

Consignment note No.:

Supplied by:

Supplied on:

(date)

Goods:

received by:	date:
checked by:	date:

Reason for complaint:

vocabulary:

defect damage

Mrs King decides to take the remaining perfect stock of recycled copy paper into storage. Accordingly, the figure shown on the warehouse stock card is increased by the quantity taken into stock.

Task 46:

Make the necessary alterations to the appropriate cards.

In the meantime, Mrs Bower from Purchasing, has received the complaints sheet. This is used as a kind of standard letter of complaint. The supplier will need to know exactly what is wrong with the goods he delivered. So the type of defect or damage will have to be described in detail. Mrs Bower decides to give this job to Mr Stain, one of the trainees.

Mrs Bower

Mr Stain

Mrs Bower: Mr Stain, our warehouse manager, Mrs King, has told me that a part of a new consignment of recycled copy paper arrived in poor condition.
Could you please have a look at the complaints sheet?

Mr Stain: Certainly, Mrs Bower. I'll look into it straightaway.

Mrs Bower: I'd like you to find out how this could have happened and what we can do to solve the problem. You will find some useful information in the info-folder at your department. There is a section covering various forms of complaint and procedures.

When you have decided on the best way to solve the problem, come back to me and we'll discuss it.

Mr Stain: OK, I'll get down to it straightaway.

Mr Stain begins, as he said, straightaway to check the complaints sheet and to read the info-folder. Under the heading 'inferior consignment' he finds a short description of different types of complaints.

vocabulary:

alteration	change
remaining	being left

MODO OFFICE SERVICE LTD.

Info-Folder: **Purchasing department**

3.4. Inferior consignments

3.4.1 Sample of a complaints sheet

The purchasing department receives the completed report directly from the warehouse.

COMPLAINTS SHEET

Supplier:	**Goods:** received by:	date:
	checked by:	date:
Consignment note No.:	Reason for complaint:	
Supplied by:		
Supplied on: (date)		

3.4.2 **Forms of defects**

Wrong **type** of goods: e.g. photocopy paper instead of writing paper.

Wrong **quantity:** e.g. too few or too many goods.

Wrong **quality:**
- Inferior standard/incorrect description of quality
  e.g. carbon paper which cannot be used more than once, although is advertised as „can be used for up to ten copies".
- Inferior quality/damage caused by bad weather, sunlight/perished goods, etc.

an extract out of the info-folder

Task 47:

Decide which defect applies in this case and explain why.

vocabulary:

Mr Stain has a close look at the contract to find out what rights his company has.

*8 Delivery, Property and Risk

(a) Subject to any agreement to the contrary in the Contract the Buyer shall be bound to accept delivery of Goods at its own premises when they are ready for delivery by the Seller.

(b) The Seller shall nor incur any liability or obligation to the Buyer in respect of any failure to deliver or delay in delivery.

(c) The risk in Goods shall pass to the Buyer when they are delivered to the Buyer or to some other person on its behalf in accordance with its instructions.

(d) Property in Goods will pass to the Buyer only when payment in full for such Goods (including any interest payable pursuant to Condition 3) has been received by the Seller.

10 Warranty and Claims

(a) All conditions and warranties whether express or implied by statute or otherwise shall be construed subject to these Conditions and insofar as they are inconsistent therewith shall be excluded.

(b) The Seller warrants only that Goods are reasonably free from defects in material or workmanship on their delivery and, if stored under conditions which are reasonable, will remain so for a period of one year from the date of delivery (the "Warranty Period").

(c) It shall be the duty of the Buyer, before using any Goods and before parting with possession of the same, to test and examine such Goods in every respect.

(d) Any complaint of short delivery must be notified to the Seller within 24 hours of receipt of Goods and confirmed in writing at that time by the Buyer to the Seller. Any complaint of failure to deliver Goods invoiced must be so notified and confirmed within ten days of the date of the invoice.

(e) Claims in respect of any alleged damage to or defect in Goods delivered must:

- (i) if the defect would have been revealed by normal examination of the outturn sheets, or by reasonable examination of such Goods on arrival, be made in writing within 14 days after delivery, or
- (ii) if related to the transport of such Goods, be made within such a time as will enable the Seller to comply with the time limits and procedures of any carriers by whom such Goods were transported, or
- (iii) otherwise be made within the Warranty Period and within 14 days of any such damage or defect becoming apparent.

(f) If the Buyer shall make any complaint within the time stipulated the Seller shall, after it has had a reasonable time to investigate the same and examine the Goods in dispute and if the Goods are defective, as its option:

- (i) replace the Goods, or
- (ii) accept the return of Goods and credit the Buyer with the price thereof, or
- (iii) make to the Buyer and allowance representing the difference between the value of the Goods at the time of the complaint by the Buyer and the value they would have had if they had not been so defective (provided that the Buyer shall still be liable to pay the balance not in dispute according to normal terms).

(g) Other than as permitted by the Seller pursuant to Condition 10(f) Goods shall not be returned by the Buyer to the Seller without prior agreement, when the Seller reserves the right to change 20 per cent of the invoice value or five pounds (whichever is greater) for handling costs.

extract of the conditions of sale (contract)

* use your dictionary to look up the unknown words

Buyer and Seller are replaced by "it" because the companies are the contractors and they aren't thought of as persons.

Task 48:

What are the rights of a buyer who is supplied with faulty goods according to the conditions of sale of Paper Mills.

Mr Stain makes a draft of the various rights a buyer has.

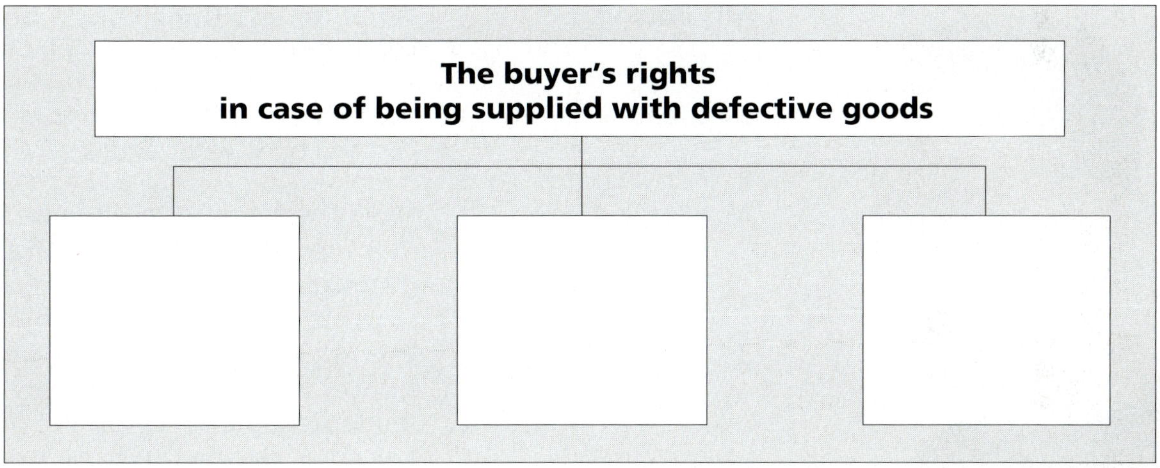

Task 49:

Which right will Mr Stain decide to make use of in this case? Explain your decision.

vocabulary:

Mr Stain presents his proposal to Mrs Bower and explains why he decided on this procedure. The conversation continues as follows:

Mrs Bower

Mr Stain

Mrs Bower:	OK, Mr Stain, I agree with your proposal. I think we have found the solution for our problem. What do you think we should do now?
Mr Stain:	I think it would be best to inform the supplier straight away.
Mrs Bower:	Right, and how should we inform them?
Mr Stain:	We will phone them – that is the quickest.
Mrs Bower:	That may be the quickest, but in order to prove the facts at a later time, we always make such complaints in writing.
Mr Stain:	Yes, I can well imagine that.
Mrs Bower:	What do you think should be included in such complaint?
Mr Stain:	Well, we must tell them that some of the cartons had water stains on them.
Mrs Bower:	Well, there is a little bit more than that. You must quote the exact number of the damaged cartons. Point out to the supplier which consignment you are talking about. You must not forget to inform him that you inspected the goods immediately on receipt. We normally give them a proposal how to solve the problem. Mr, Stain, could you make a draft of such a letter?

Task 50:

Draft the letter of complaint to Paper Mills plc. Use the blank letter heading (see page 72).

V *vocabulary:*

to include	to involve
proposal	suggestion
to prove	to show that something is right
to quote	to indicate

Substitution Table (complaint)

Salutation (see page 23)

We	are sorry regret having	to	tell inform advise	you	that	your	shipment consignment delivery	dated of	2nd March 24th July	has not	met come up to	our	approval. expectations.
											turned out to our satisfaction. been up to our standards.		
										has given cause for complaint.			

On When While	examining checking	the	articles goods products	we	noticed found discovered	that	some of them					arrived in a badly damaged condition.		
							the items	quoted indicated	below on the	list paper	enclosed attached	were	completely partly slightly badly	damaged. stained. broken. torn.
													missing.	
													damaged	by water. during transport. in transit.

We	think believe suppose	that	the damage	is due to was caused by results from	careless rough unskilled	handling	during	(un)loading. transport.
							at the docks. in the warehouse.	
There is no doubt Evidently Obviously Apparently					inadequate poor insufficient improper a mistake in	packing.		

We	are not willing refuse	to	accept keep	the	goods items articles	supplied	unless you	grant us a considerable reduction in price. reduce the price considerably.

We	have no use can't make any use	of the articles you sent us and are	placing them at your disposal. holding them for your instructions.

We shall expect you to	devote more care to the execution of our orders		in future.
	avoid	similar occurences a repetition of the trouble	in future.
	credit us for the damaged goods.		
	settle this matter	to our complete satisfaction. satisfactorily.	
	send us replacements for the damaged goods	immediately. by return of post.	

Complimentary close (see page 23)

V ***vocabulary:***

to advise	to recommend something to somebody	insufficient	not enough
to devote	to give one's time, energy, etc. to someone	occurence	event, incident
to place something at somebody's disposal	to let somebody have something	to regret	to fell sorry about something
to be due to	caused by something or somebody	replacement	something sent in exchange for something else
evidently	oviously	to result from	to occur as an effect from something else
		rough	not smooth, using force
		to settle	to arrange something finally

By Appointment to
HM the Queen
Paper Merchants

MoDo

MoDo
Office Service Ltd
Office Papers

Rosemount Avenue
West Byfleet
SURREY KT14 6LE
Tel 0932 335577
Fax 0932 335580

Printed on Datacopy Laser Wove 90g/m²

BS5750

MoDo Office Service Ltd
A member of the MoDo Group
Registered Office Rosemount Avenue West Byfleet
SURREY KT14 6LE Registered in England 1097405

Mr Stain shows Mrs Bower the draft of the letter. After making a few corrections, she gives the draft back to Mr Stain and asks him to write it on the PC. After checking the letter a second time, she signs it and has it posted.

13 June

Paper Mills plc react promptly to the complaint by sending a fax. Mrs Bower compares it to our letter of 10 June. Should any objection be in the fax, we can contact the supplier immediately. Otherwise all we have to do is to wait for the replacement consignment.

PAPER MILLS PLC

12 Kings Road, Hersham, SURREY KT12 5FH
Tel.: 0932 831578
Fax: 0932 831590

FAX

DATE: 13 June 19
TIME:

TO: **Modo Office Service Ltd.**
Rosemount Avenue
West Byfleet
SURREY
KT14 6LE

TEL.:
FAX:

MODO Received: 13 June
for:
☐ Managing Director
☒ Purchasing Department
☐ Sales Department
☐ Warehouse Department
☐ Administration Department

FROM:
TEL.:
FAX:

SUBJECT: Your letter of complaint

CC:

Number of pages: 1

MESSAGE:

Dear Sirs

We regret that 6 cartons of the consignment No. 2434 were not in order. The replacement and the collection of the damaged cartons will be carried out as soon as possible.

Yours faithfully

Robert Redman

fax sent by Paper Mills plc

Task 51:

Compare the fax with our complaint of 10 June. Were our requests accepted and fulfilled?

vocabulary:

15 June

The replacement consignment has arrived.

Task 52:

Check and see whether the consignment corresponds to the consignment note and the fax.

PAPER MILLS PLC

12 Kings Road
Hersham
SURREY
KT12 5FH
Tel.: 0932 831578
Fax: 0932 831590

MoDo Office Service Ltd
Rosemount Avenue
West Byfleet
SURREY KT12 6LE

Consignment Note - Customer Copy

Date of Despatch	Customer No.	Our Order No.	Date of Order	Document No.
15 June	19230	3921	9 June	2 448 783

Quantity	Unit	Description	Weight
15	@ 1,000	Recycled copy paper -grey- A4 Article No. 4001	42 kg
		Total weight	42 kg
		Add 5% for packaging	2.1 kg

Received the above in good condition

Signature

Name

goods received and checked: Smith
Date 15 June
Date Signature Smith

All goods supplied to the Company's conditions of sale

consignment note received from Paper Mills plc

The arrival of the goods must now be entered in the warehouse stock card.

Task 53:

Complete the warehouse stock card.

21 June

The invoice for the ordered recycled copy paper has arrived today and needs to be checked and settled.

PAPER MILLS PLC

12 Kings Road
Hersham

SURREY
KT12 5FH

Tel.: 0932 831578
Fax: 0932 831590

MODO Received:
for:
☐ Managing Director
☒ Purchasing Department
☐ Sales Department
☐ Warehouse Department
☒ Administration Department

MoDo Office Service Ltd
Rosemount Avenue
West Byfleet
SURREY KT12 6LE

Sales invoice

Customer's order number	Our Order No.	Supplying Sales Office	Customer No.	Invoice Date	Invoice No.	Page
	3921	Hersham	19230	13 June 19..	199-009-7	1

Quantity	Description	Size	Subs	Weight/Unit	Price £/Unit	Qty. Disc %	Value
500	Recycled copy paper -grey-	A4		2.8 kg	4.18	3 %	2,027.30

checked and approved:
BOWER
Date: 21 June
Signature: Bower

VAT % Rate	Goods Value	VAT Value
17.5	2,027.30	354.78

Goods Total £ 2,027.30
VAT Total £ 354.78
Invoice Total £ 2,382.08

TERMS NET 30 DAYS

invoice received from Paper Mills plc

E

Exercises:

Answer the following questions.

1. Which amount can the price of the goods be reduced by?

2. What is added to the net price of the goods?

3. Where were the goods despatched?

4. When has payment to be effected?

Task 54:

Work out the sum which has to be transferred. Deduct the cash discount and fill in the cheque.

cheque

Task 55:

Note the date of the invoice and the date of payment on the purchase stock card. The case is now finished.

At work

You have been working for MODO for the past few months and have carried out various forms of commercial work.

You have added a new product to the company's range. You have been dealing with the process of purchasing from making an enquiry to writing a complaint.

Task 56:

Make a presentation of the business procedures which are discussed in this book.

a) Make your presentation either in writing or as a diagramm to show what you and your fellow students have learned. Use a wall chart or slides and an overhead projector.

b) Discuss the presented material and decide whether the presentation has been done correctly.

While working with this book you have learned a lot about the day-to-day running of a business and you know now how your fellow students react to the different situations.

Task 57:

Evaluate what you did in your class.

a) Discuss th

16 Sept

Pat Green, the manager of the purchasing department, has visited the Paris Paper Fair and received two very interesting offers from Finish and Russian suppliers who sell recycled photocopy paper at especially favourable conditions.

She informs Mrs Painter, the managing director, about the two offers and all the novelties presented at the fair and suggests to call in a meeting to discuss the matter with the managers of the other departments. Mrs Painter asks Mrs Green to photocopy the two offers she got at the fair and to pass them on to the managers of all departments so that they can have a look at them before the meeting.

In addition to that she asks Mrs Green to make a comparison of the two offers in British pounds.

RUSSIAN PAPER FACTORY Ltd.

51, Dalne vostochny pr.
St. Petersburg, 19 32 24
Russia

10 September 19..

Your ref.: PG/JB Our ref.:

Dear Sirs,

We heard from one of our agents in England that you are interested in buying photocopy paper.
Here in Russia we have become one of the main producers and distributors of all sorts of paperware.
We intend to extend our business to the western parts of Europe. To gain a foothold on the British market we have reduced our prices by about 20% in order to compensate the imposed import duty. Should we become business partners and the turnover is good, I am sure that we will be able to accommodate your wishes regarding quality and price.

The valid prices for photocopy paper (recycled) are:

A4887	A4	white per 1000 sheets	$ 3.30
A4890	A4	green per 1000 sheets	$ 3.25
A4891	yellow		
A4892	red		
A4893	blue		
A3887	A3	white per 500 sheets	$ 3.15
A3890	green		
A3891	yellow		
A3892	red		
A3893	blue		
	A3	all colours as above per 500 sheets	$ 3.20

The prices are to be understood DDP West Byfleet for orders of a minimum of 100,000 sheets A4 or 50,000 sheets A3.
Time of delivery 6-8 weeks after receipt of order.
Terms of payment 30 D/S with irrevocable letter of credit made out in our favour, for payment within 14 days we grant 2 % cash discount.
As already mentioned should our business develop to our mutual satisfaction, other terms can be arranged.
We look forward to the pleasure of serving you and you can rest assured that your orders will be given our best attention.

Very truly yours

Pavel Kheifets
Sales manager

Russian Paper Factory Ltd. 51, Dalne vostochny pr. St. Petersburg, 193224

P&C MILLS PORI (Björneborg)

Björneborg - Finland

Kirkkokatu 17 • 90 200 Björneborg 12

MODO OFFICE SERVICE LTD
Rosemount Avenue
West Byfleet
SURREY
KT14 6LE

9 September 19..

Your ref.: PG/JB Our ref.: PH/NM

Dear Sirs

On the occasion of the Paris Paper Fair we met the manager of your purchasing department, Pat Green, who told us that you are interested in buying recycled photocopy paper. We are pleased to submit the following offer:

25674	papers A4	80 g.	1000 sheets	white	£ 2.80
25680	"	"	"	red	£ 2.95
25681	"	"	"	blue	£ 2.95
25682	"	"	"	green	£ 2.95

All A4 papers are to be understood as recycled.

34444	papers A3	80 g.	1000 sheets	white	£ 4.80
34450	"	"	"	red	£ 4.90
34451	"	"	"	blue	£ 4.90
34452	"	"	"	green	£ 4.90

All papers A3 are to be understood as recycled.

As one of the main producers of paper and board as well as other printing accessories in Finland we are able to supply at very short notice.
We can grant you a special introductory discount of 10 % on all orders of a minimum of 100,000 sheets A4 or 50,000 sheets A3 received by 3rd June 19... Our terms of payment are 3 % within eight days. We deliver DEQ Harwich.*
We hope to hear from you soon.

Yours faithfully

Per Hakkinen

Per Hakkinen

i

Incoterms

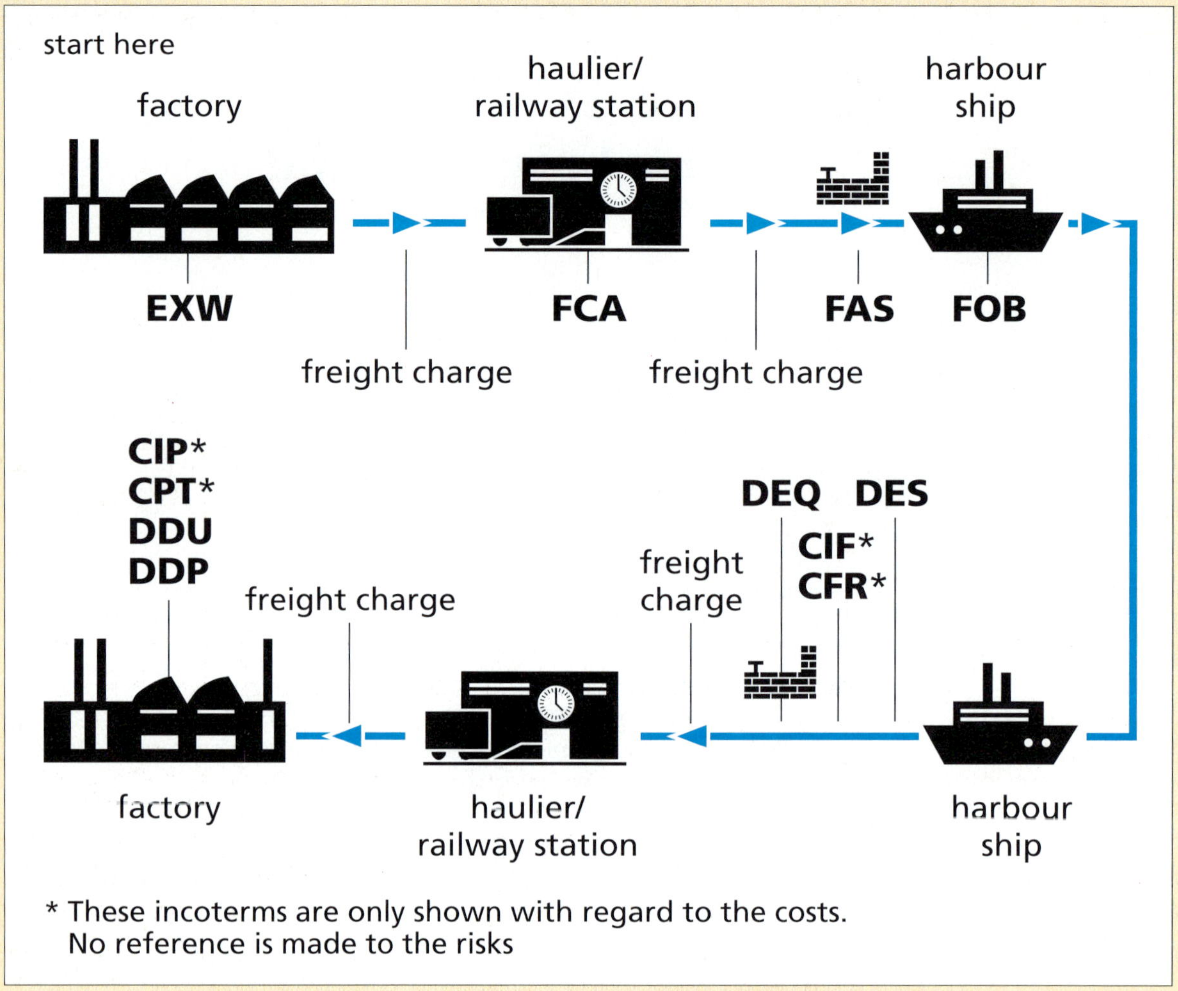

EXW	Ex Works	(... named place)
FCA	Free Carrier	(... named place)
FAS	Free Alongside Ship	(... named port of shipment)
FOB	Free On Board	(... named port of shipment)
DES	Delivered Ex Ship	(... named port of destination)
CIF	Cost, Insurance and Freight	(... named port of destination)
CFR	Cost and Freight	(... named port of destination)
DEQ	Delivered Ex Quay	(... named port of destination)
CIP	Carriage and Insurance Paid To	(... named place of destination)
CPT	Carriage Paid To	(... named place of destination)
DDU	Delivered Duty Unpaid	(... named place of destination)
DDP	Delivered Duty Paid	(... named place of destination)

V

vocabulary:

haulier	person whose job it is to transport goods

Task 58:

Convert the prices given into British pounds taking into consideration the information below on the conversion of currencies. Ask your bank about foreign exchange rates or have a look at your daily newspaper.

Because of the weakness of the Rouble, the Russians have submitted their offer in American dollars.

Conversion of currencies

In Germany, the currency exchange rates are quoted as prices, but in England they are quoted as quantities. The prices are quoted in DM for 100 units of the foreign currency (if the single unit of the currency is of a lower value than the DEM) or one unit of the foreign currency.

Example:

The exchange rate in London for German marks is 2.15 which means for £ 1.00 one has to pay DM 2.15.

Converting Pound Sterling into another currency

Example:

Work out how many $ you would get for £ 275.00 at an exchange rate of £ 1.00 = $ 1.63

$$\text{£ } 1.00 = \$ \, 1.63$$

$$\text{£ } 275 = x$$

$$x = \frac{1.63 \cdot 275}{1.00} = \$ \, 440.25$$

Converting a foreign currency into Pound Sterling in London

Example:

Work out how many Pounds Sterling you would get for DM 1,881.25 at the exchange rate of DEM 2.15 = £ 1.00

$$\text{DM } 2.15 = \text{£ } 1.00$$

$$\text{DM } 1{,}881.25 = x \text{ £}$$

$$x = \frac{1 \cdot 1{,}881.25}{2.15} = \text{£ } 875.00$$

1 · foreign currency

Task 59:

Make a comparison of the two offers based on the purchase of 100,000 sheets by filling in the table below.

MODO OFFICE SERVICE LTD., West Byfleet, SURREY

Comparison of offers

Article No:	Article:	Date:
Supplier: Offer of: Order quantity:		
I. Quantity comparison list purchase price less discount	£	£
= target purchase price less supplier's cash discount		
= cash purchase price + packing costs + transport costs		
= PURCHASE PRICE		
II. Quality comparison: minimum order quantity		
time of delivery		
after sales service		
further quality criteria		
order from		

Task 60:

Decide which offer is the most favourable one. Give reasons.

The managers discuss whether it would be worthwhile buying recycled photocopy paper from abroad.

Task 61:

Play the roles given in the role play in the appendix. Use the cues when arguing (or making) your points.

The managers decide to order from abroad.

Task 62:

Place the order per fax.

FAX

MoDo

MoDo
Office Service Ltd
Office Papers

Rosemount Avenue
West Byfleet
SURREY KT14 6LE
Tel 0932 335577
Fax 0932 335580

DATE: TIME:
TO: TEL.:

FAX:
FROM: TEL.:

SUBJECT:
CC:
Number of pages:
MESSAGE:

VOCABULARY

English	German	French	Spanish
A			
above	oben	ci-dessus	arriba
accessoires	Zubehör	les accessoires	los accesorios
to accompany	begleiten	accompagner	acompañar
according to	gemäß	suite à	según
accordingly	gemäß	selon	según y como
accounting	Buchhaltung	la compabilité	la contabilidad
to act out	ausführen	exécuter	ejecutar
to add	hinzufügen	ajouter	añadir
addition	Hinzufügung	l'addition	la adición
additional	zusätzlich	supplémentaire	aditivo
to be adhered to	angehören	faire partie de	pertenecer a
administration	Verwaltung	l'administration (f.)	la administración
administration department	Verwaltungsabteilung	le service d'administration	el servicio de administración
advertising	Werbung	la publicité	la publicidad
affair	Geschäft	l'affaire (f.)	el negocio
aforesaid	vorhergesagt	prévu,e	previsto
aim	Ziel	le but	la meta
amicable	freundschaftlich	amical,e	amistoso
amount	Betrag	le montant	la suma
anniversary	Geburtstag	l'anniversaire (m.)	el cumpleaños
appendix	Anhang	l'appendice (m.)	el apéndice
applicable	anwendbar	applicable	aplicable
apprentice	Auszubildender	l'apprenti (m.)	el aprendiz
appropriate	angemessen	approprié,e	apropiado
approximately	ungefähr	environ	aproximadamente
arbitration	Schlichtung	l'arbitrage (m.)	el arbitraje
assorted	sortiert	assorti,e	clasificar, ordenar
to be attached to	hinzugefügt sein	être attaché,e à	ser añadido
available	verfügbar	disponible	disponible
to avoid	vermeiden	éviter	evitar
B			
barrel	Fass	le tonneau	el tonel
below	unter	ci-dessous	debajo de
bill of exchange	Wechsel	la lettre de change la traite	la letra de cambio
bi- or multi-lateral	zwei- oder mehrseitig	bi- ou multilatéral,e	bi o multilateral
binding	bindend	obligatoire	obligatorio
biro	Kugelschreiber	le stylo à bille	el bolígrafo
blockage	Papierstau	le blockage	la bloqueada
to be borne	getragen werden	être à la charge de	ser cargado a
to be bound to	verpflichtet sein	être obligé,e de	
branch			

English	German	French	Spanish
C			
caller	Anrufer	la personne qui appelle	el interlocutor telefónico
to cancel	widerrufen	annuler	anular
cancellation	Widerruf	l'annulation (f.)	la anulación
capacity	Fähigkeit	la capacité	la capacidad
carbon copy paper	Durchschlagpapier	le papier carbone	el papel de carbón
cardboard box	Pappkarton	le carton	la caja de cartón
caretaker	Hausmeister	le concierge	el conserje
carriage forward	unfrei	port dû	puerto franco
carriage paid	frachtfrei	port payé	puerto pagado
cartage	Rollgeld	le camionage, le factage	gastos de camionaje
cash discount	Skonto	l'escompte (m.)	el descuento
case	Fall	le cas	el caso
category	Kategorie	la catégorie	la categoría
to cause	verursachen	causer	causar
cause	Grund	la raison	la razón
to charge	belasten	débiter	cargo
clerk	Angestellter	l'employé de bureau	el ofcinista
circular	Rundschreiben	le circulaire	le circular
coin	Münze	la pièce de monnaie	la moneda
colleague	Kollege	le, la collègue	el/la colega
to collect	(ein-) sammeln	ramasser	coleccionar
column	Spalte	la colonne	la columna
commercial	wirtschaftlich	commercial,e	comercial
common	gemeinsam	commun,e	común
to compare	vergleichen	comparer	comparar
comparison	Vergleich	la comparaison	la comparación
competitor	Wettbewerber	le concurrent,e	el competidor
complaint	Mängelrüge	la lettre de réclamation	la reclamación
completion	Vervollständigung	le complément	el completamiento
comlimentary close	Grußformel	la formule de politesse	la formula de cortesia
to compose	zusammenstellen	composer	componer
concerning	betreffend	concernant	con referencia a
to conclude	abschließen	conclure	concluir
conclusion	Abschluß	la conclusion	la conclusión
to confirm	bestätigen	confirmer	confirmar
confirmation	Bestätigung	la confirmation	la confirmación
to confiscate	beschlagnahmen	confisquer	confiscar
to consider	betrachten	considérer	considerar
considerable	beträchtlich	considérable	considerable
consideration	Betracht	la considération	la consideración
consignee	Empfänger	le destinataire	el/la destinatario/a
consignment	Sendung	l'envoi (m.)	el envío
consignor	Absender	l'expéditeur (m.)	el expedidor
continually	ständig	continuellement	continuo
contract	Vertrag	le contrat	el contrato

English	German	French	Spanish
county	Grafschaft	le comté, le département	el condado
crate	Lattenkiste	la caisse à claire-voie le cageot	la caja
cellulose	Zellulose	la cellulose	la celulosa
to check	überprüfen	examiner	examinar
clause	Klausel	la clause	la claúsula
criteria	Kriterien	les critères	los criterios
customer	Kunde	le client	el cliente
D			
data	Daten	les données	los datos
to decide	beschließen	décider	decidir
to decrease	abnehmen	baisser	disminuir
to deduct	ableiten, -ziehen	déduire	deducir
to deem	denken, meinen	penser	pensar
to deliver	liefern	livrer	suministrar
delivery	Lieferung	la livraison	el suministro
demand	Nachfrage	la demande	la demanda
department	Abteilung	le département	el departamento
to describe	beschreiben	décrire	describir
to derive from	ableiten	dériver de	derivar de
destination	Ziel	la destination	el destino
discretion	Diskretion	la disrétion	la discreción
despatch	Versand	l'expédition	la expedición
despatch note	Lieferschein	le récépissé de livraison	el talón/la nota de entrega
dispute	Streit	la dispute	la disputa
dissatisfaction	Unzufriedenheit	la dissatisfaction	el descontento
distinction	Unterschied	la distinction	la diferencia
dozen	Dutzend	la douzaine	la docena
doubt	Zweifel	la doute	la duda
draft	Entwurf	la brouillon	el bosquejo
drop in	Fall (z.B. des Preises)	la baisse	la baja
drum	Fass	le fût, le tonneau	juntar
to be due	fällig sein	être dû,e	ser pagadero
dust	Staub	la poussière	el polvo
dust-free	staubfrei	sans poussière	sin polvo
E			
employee	Angestellter	l'employé (m.)	el empleado
enclosures	Anlagen	les pièces jointes	las piezas juntas
without engagement	freibleibend	sans engagement	precio facultativo
enquiry	Anfrage	la demande d'offre	la demanda de oferta
to ensure	versichern	assurer	asegurar
environmentally	Umwelt-	écologique	[illegible]
[illegible]			

English	German	French	Spanish
to estimate	schätzen	estimer	estimar
examination	Prüfung	l'examen	el examen
excerpt	Ausschnitt	l'extrait (m.)	el extracto
to exhibit	ausstellen	exposer	exponer
to expire	auslaufen	expirer	expirar
extent	Ausmaß	l'importance, la mesure	la impotancia, la medida
external	extern	extérieur,se	exterior
ex quay	ab Kai	de quai à	muelle franco
ex works	ab Werk	départ usine	a partir de fábrica
eye-catching	auffallend	frappant,e	sorprendente
F			
fair	Messe	la foire	la feria
faithfully	getreu	fidèlement	fielmente
fee	Gebühr	les droits	los derechos
fellow	Kamerad	le type	el colega
felt&fibre pens	Filz- und Faserstifte	le feutre	la fibra, plumones/ el rotulador
freight	Fracht	le fret	el flete
friction	Bruch	la friction	la infracción
to fulfil	erfüllen	accomplir	completar
fulfilment	Erfüllung	l'accomplissement (m.)	el cumplimiento
furniture	Möbel	le meuble	el mueble
G			
to gain	gewinnen	gagner	ganar
at a glance	auf einen Blick	d'un coup d'oeil	a simple vista
to grant	gewähren	accorder	conceder
greeting	Gruß	la salutation	el saludo
gross	brutto	brut	bruto
to guarantee	garantieren	garantir	garantizar
H			
handling charges	Bearbeitungsgebühr	frais de traitement	la factura de camionaje
harbour	Hafen	le port	el puerto
haulier	Frachtführer	l'entrepreneur de transport	el conductor de transporte
heading	Titel	le titre	el título
to hire	leihen	emprunter	prestar
I			
illegally	ungesetzlich	illégal,e	ilegal
immediately	sofort	immédiatement	inmediatamente
implements	Werkzeuge	les outils	las herramientas
to imply	einschließen	impliquer	implicado
to increase	erhöhen	augmenter	aumentar
increasingly	immer mehr	de plus en plus	más y más

English	German	French	Spanish
influence	Einfluß	l'influence (f.)	la influencia
to influence	beeinflussen	influencer	influenciar
initial	anfänglich	initial,e	iniciador/a
ink-jet printers	Tintenstrahldrucker	l'imprimante à jet d'encre	la impresora
interest rate	Zinssatz	le taux d'intérêt	la tasa de interes
invariably	unveränderlich	invariablement	invariable
invoice	Rechnung	la facture	la factura
to involve	einschließen	inclure	incluir
to issue	herausgeben	émettre	emitir
issue	Ausgabe	l'émission, l'édition (f.)	la emisión, la edición
J			
to judge	beurteilen	juger	juzgar
jurisdiction	Rechtssprechung	la juridiction	la jurisdicción
K			
knowledge	Kenntnis	la connaissance	el conocimiento
L			
lateral	seitlich, Seiten-	latéral,e	lateral
layout	Layout	la mise en pages	la disposición, el plan
lead pencil	Bleistift	le crayon	el lápiz
legally	legal	légal,e	legal
liability	Verpflichtung	l'obligation (f.)	la obligación
local	örtlich	local,e	local
lorry	LKW	le camion	el camión
loss	Verlust	la perte	la pérdida
lump sum price	Pauschalpreis	le prix forfaitaire	el precio
M			
mail order house	Versandhaus	la maison de vente par correspondance	las casa de expedición
main	Haupt-	principal,e	principal
manner	Art	la sorte	la clase
to be marked with	gekennzeichnet sein mit	être marqué, e de	ser mercado con
marking	Kennzeichnung	la marquage	la marca
to match	passen, entsprechen	correspondre à	corresponder a
in the meantime	in der Zwischenzeit	entretemps	entre tiempo
to measure	messen	mesurer	medir
measure	Maß	la mesure	la medida
to mention	erwähnen	mentionner	mencionar
Messrs	Herren, Firma	Messieurs	los señores
mid-term	mittelfristig	à moyen terme	a por termino medio
mill	Mühle	le moulin	el molino
mutually	gegenseitig	mutuellement	mutualmente

English	German	French	Spanish
N			
necessary	notwendig	nécessaire	necesario
to notify	bekanntmachen	signaler, aviser	señalar, avisar
nowadays	heutzutage	à présent	hoy en día
O			
obliged	verpflichtet	obligé,e	obligado a
to obtain	erhalten	obtenir	obtener
to occur	passieren, auftreten	avoir lieu	tener lugar
offer	Angebot	l'offre	la oferta
offset paper	Offsetpapier	le papier offset	el papel offset
opening	Anfang	le début	el comienzo
opinion	Meinung	l'avis (m.)	el aviso
orally	mündlich	oralement	oralmente
outdoor service	Außendienst	le service externe	el servicio de difusión
overdraft	Überziehung	le découvert	el descubierto de una cuenta
overdue	überfällig	en souffrance	vencido y no pagado
ownership	Eigentum	la properiété	la propiedad
P			
packing	Verpackung	l'emballage (m.)	el embalaje
paper sacks	Papiersäcke	les sacs en papier	el saco de papel
parcel	Paket	le colis	el paquete
parent company	Muttergesellschaft	la société mère	la sociedad matriz
percentage	Prozentsatz	le pourcentage	el porcentaje
to permit	erlauben	permettre	permitir
persuasive	überredend	persuadant,e	persuasivo a
phrases	Ausdrücke	les expressions (f.)	las expresiones
polite	höflich	poli,e	amable
possession	Besitz	la possession	la posesión
to preceed	vorausgehen	précéder	preceder
pre-payment	Vorauszahlung	le paiement par avance	el pago anticipado
to prevent	verhindern	empêcher	prevenir
price reduction	Preisreduzierung	la réduction de prix	la reducción de precios
procedure	Vorgang	la procédure	el procedimiento
process	Prozess	le procès	el proceso
profit charge	Gewinnzuschlag	la marge bénéficiaire	la ganancia adicional
to promulgate	öffentlich bekanntmachen	annoncer publiquement	anunciar
property	Eigentum	la propriété	la propiedad
proposal	Vorschlag	la proposition	la proposición
to protect	schützen	protéger	proteger
to provide	liefern	livrer	proveer
punctuation	Zeichensetzung	la ponctuation	la punctuación
pupil	Schüler	l'élève	el alumno
purchase	Kauf	l'achat	la compra

English	German	French	Spanish
purchase movements card	Einkaufspendelkarte	la carte de l'achat mouvante	la tarjeta de compra movible
purchase stock card	Einkaufsstammkarte	la carte de l'achat originaire	la tarjeta de compra original
purchasing department	Einkaufsabteilung	le service d'achat	el departamento de compras
to put a caller through	einen Anrufer durch-stellen	passer une personne à la personne à l'appareil	pasar de una persona a la otra
Q			
quantity	Menge	la quantité	la cantidad
to quote	angeben	indiquer	indicar
R			
rags	Lumpen	la guenille	el trapo
range	Verkaufsprogramm	la gamme	el programa de ventas
reaction	Reaktion	la réaction	la reacción
rebate	Rabatt	le rabais	la rebaja
recipient	Empfänger	le destinataire	el destinatario
to recommend	empfehlen	recommander	recomendar
recommendation	Empfehlung	la recommandation	la recomendación
recycled	recycled	recycler, récupérer	recuperador
to refer to	sich beziehen auf	se référer à	referirse a
reference	Bezug	la référence	la referencia
reference line	Bezugszeichenzeile	les références (f.)	las referencias
to refuse	ablehnen	refuser	rechazar
to regard	betrachten	considérer, regarder	mirar
with regard to	im Hinblick auf	en considération de	en consideración a
to regulate	regulieren	régler	regular
reliable	zuverlässig	sérieux, sur qui l'on peut compter	de absoluta confianza
to remain	bleiben	rester	quedar
remark	bemerken	remarquer	recordar
reminder	Zahlungserinnerung	la lettre de rappel	recordar el pago
reply	Antwort	la réponse	la respuesta
report	Bericht	le rapport	el reportaje
representative	Vertreter	le représentant	el representante
to request	bitten	demander	pedir
request	Bitte	la demande	la demanda
on request	auf Anfrage	sur demande	a petición
to require	benötigen	requérir, avoir besoin de	necesitar
requirement	Erfordernis	l'exigence (f.)	la exigencia
responsible	verantwortlich	responsable	responsable
retail trade	Einzelhandel	le commerce de détail	el comercio al detalle
S			
salary	Gehalt	le salaire	[illegible]

English	German	French	Spanish
sales department	Verkaufsabteilung	le service de ventes	el servicio de ventas
sales movement	Umsatzänderung	le changement de chiffre d'affaires	el cambio de ganancias
sample	Muster, Probe	l'échantillon (m.)	la muestra
a large scale order	ein Großauftrag	une commande importante	una orden importante
to serve	dienen	servir	servir
shade	Farbton	la nuance, le ton	e color, el tono
sheet	Blatt	la feuille	la hoja
to be short of something	jemandem mangelt es an etwas	avoir besoin de	necesitar algo
sincerely	ernsthaft	sérieusement	seriamente
sinking	sinkend	en baisse	la baja
size	Größe	la taille, les dimensions	la talla, la medida
sketch	Skizze, Entwurf	le croquis, l'ébauche	el dibujo, el bosquejo
sole property	alleiniges Eigentum	la properiété unique	el único propietario
solicited offer	verlangtes Angebot	une offre sollicitée	la oferta solicitada
to solve	lösen	résoudre	resolver
source	Quelle	la source	la fuente
space	Raum	l'espace (m.)	el espacio
staff	Personal, Angestellte	le personnel	el personal
to stagnate	stagnieren	stagner	estagnar
to state	feststellen	constater	constatar
stationery	Büromaterial	le matérial de bureau	el material de oficina
stock	Lager	le stock	el almacenamiento
stock manager	Lagerleiter	le chef de magasin	el jefe de
to store	lagern	emmagasiner, stocker	almacenamiento, almacenar
straightaway	geradewegs	immédiatement	inmediatamente
straightforward	geradeaus	franc, simple	directo
subject heading	Betreff	l'object (m.)	jefe subordinado
subject to our final confirmation	freibleibend	sans engagement	sujeto a nuestra confirmación final
subject to the goods being unsold	Zwischenverkauf vorbehalten	sauf vente entretemps	intermediario de ventas restringido
subject to price revision	Preisänderungen vorbehalten	sous réserve de modifications de prix	el cambio de precios con restricción
substitution	Ersetzen	la substitution, le replacement	la substitución
substitution table	Satzbautafel	le tableau de substitution	la substitución de mesa
to succeed	Erfolg haben	avoir du succès	tener éxito
to suggest	vorschlagen	proposer	proponer
suggestion	Vorschlag	la proposition	la proposición
suitable	passend	approprié,e	apropiado/a
supplier	Lieferant	le fournisseur	el suministrador
supply	Lieferung	la livraison	el suministro
to supply	liefern	livrer	suministrar
support	Unterstützung	le support	el apoyo

English	German	French	Spanish
T			
task	Aufgabe	la tâche	la tarea
telephone answering machine	Anrufbeantworter	le répondeur	el contestador automático
terms of delivery	Lieferungsbedingungen	les conditions de livraison	las condiciones de suministro
terms of payment	Zahlungsbedingungen	les conditions de paiement	las condiciones de pago
trainee	Auszubildender	l'apprenti (m.)	el aprendiz
transaction	Transaktion	la transaction	la transacción
transparent	durchsichtig	transparent,e	transparente
trial order	Probeauftrag	l'ordre d'essai	la order de prueba
turnover	Umsatz	le chiffre d'affaires	las operaciones comerciales
U			
unconditionally	bedingungslos	inconditionnellement	incondicionalmente
undermentioned	unten genannt	mentionné,e ci-dessous	abajo mencionado/a
upwards	nach oben, aufwärts	à partir de, dès, et plus	a partir de, y mas
V			
valid	gültig	valable	válido/a
validity	Gültigkeit	la validité	la validez
value	Wert	la valeur	el valor
value added tax	Mehrwertsteuer	la taxe sur la valeur ajoutée	el impuesto de valor adjuntado/a
various	verschieden	varié,e	variado/a
vehicle	Fahrzeug	le véhicule	el vehículo
virtually	tatsächlich	en fait	en hecho
W			
warehouse	Lager	le magasin	el almacén
warehouse stock card	Lagerbestandskarte	la carte de stockage	la tarjeta de almacenamiento
waste paper	Altpapier	les vieux papiers	los papeles viejos
watermark	Wasserzeichen	le filigrane	el filigrana
withdrawal	Abzug	le retrait	el descuento, el retraso
wholesale company	Großhandelsfirma	l'entreprise de gros	el comercio al por mayor
wood-free	holzfrei	sans bois	sin madera
worth	Wert	la valeur	el valor

The cards provided for role playing can be used for Task 61 on page 83.
Make sure that each actor uses the cues given.
Additional information can be used.

The vocabulary games on pp. 98 - 101 can be played in groups.
They refer to the vocabulary given in this book.
Game No. 1 is to be played after p. 22, Game No. 2 after p. 34, Game No. 3 after p. 46 and Game No. 4 after all the rest.
If there are any doubts you can also have a look at the vocabulary in the appendix.

ROLE PLAY

Pat Green
Purchasing Department

Cues:

price
standard
...

Tom More
Sales Department

Cues:

qualitiy
punctuality
costs
...

Paul Lovecake
Administration Department

Cues:

method of payment
correspondence
place of jurisdiction
...

Elizabeth Painter
Managing Director

Cues:

problems
payment

GAME 33 No 1 (dominoes)

Instructions

First of all make a copy of the vocabulary.

Cut the words out making sure that you have the English word on the left and the German one on the right, both words must be on the same slip.

example: company Angestellte

Mix up the slips and ask your fellow students to stand in a circle in groups of three or four with each person holding one of the slips. Make sure that each slip translates correctly both to the left and to the right.

example: company Angestellte | employee Lieferanten | suppliers Gebiet

It does not matter which slip you begin with, if you lay the slips correctly you will form a circle.

company	Angestellte	employee	Lieferanten	suppliers	Gebiet
area	Kunde	customer	Produkte	products	Auszubildender
trainee	Möbel	furniture	Schreibwaren	stationery	Ziel
aim	sortiert	assorted	Papierstau	blockage	Blatt
sheet	holzfrei	wood-free	Mitarbeiter	colleague	Anfrage
enquiry	Umsatz	turnover	Kugelschreiber	biro	erlauben
to permit	gegenseitig	mutual	schätzen	to estimate	Verzeichnis
directory	Vorschlag	proposal	Ausschnitt	excerpt	beschreiben
to describe	Landkarte	map	Einzelhandel	retail	Verpackung
packing	gemeinsam	common	Proben	samples	Anlagen

GAME 33 No 2 (dominoes)

Instructions

First of all make a copy of the vocabulary.

Cut the words out making sure that you have the English word on the left and the German one on the right, both words must be on the same slip.

example: | company Angestellte |

Mix up the slips and ask your fellow students to stand in a circle in groups of three or four with each person holding one of the slips. Make sure that each slip translates correctly both to the left and to the right.

example: | cwo Gesellschaft | ↔ | company Angestellte | ↔ | employee Lieferant |

It does not matter which slip you begin with, if you lay the slips correctly you will form a circle.

supplier	Fass	barrel	Fall/Kiste	case	Dutzend
dozen	Adresse	address	Briefkopf	letterhead	Bezugszeichen
reference line	Brief	letter	Anfrage	enquiry	Daten
data	Angebot	offer	Angestellter	clerk	Korbflasche
carboy	Empfänger	consignee	Lattenkiste	crate	Absender
consignor	Datum	date	Bleistift	pencil	prüfen
to check	sofort	straight away	Stempel	stamp	erhalten
to receive	kostenpauschal	lump sum	Wert	value	Wechsel
bill of exchange	gültig	valid	überfällig	overdue	Gesetz
law	angeben	to quote	gelb	yellow	Skonto

GAME 33 No 3 (dominoes)

Instructions

First of all make a copy of the vocabulary.
Cut the words out making sure that you have the English word on the left and the German one on the right, both words must be on the same slip.

example: | company Angestellte |

Mix up the slips and ask your fellow students to stand in a circle in groups of three or four with each person holding one of the slips. Make sure that each slip translates correctly both to the left and to the right.

example: | cwo Gesellschaft | company Angestellte | employee Lieferant |

It does not matter which slip you begin with, if you lay the slips correctly you will form a circle.

ship	Streit	dispute	anwendbar	applicable	transportieren
to transport	Ausgabe	issue	bar	cash	Anzahlung
deposit	Handel	trade	Hilfe	aid/help	Kunde
customer	Aufgabe	task	Kriterien	criteria	sofort
immediately	Einkauf	purchase	Gewinn	profit	Skonto
discount	Berechnung	calculation	Rabatt	rebate	mündlich
oral	Datum	date	Verkäufer	seller	Bemerkung
remark	schreiben	to write	Beschreibung	description	Seite
page	unter	below	Blatt	sheet	widerrufen
to cancel	Branche	branch	Verwaltung	administration	ab Kai

GAME 33 No 4 (dominoes)

Instructions

First of all make a copy of the vocabulary.

Cut the words out making sure that you have the English word on the left and the German one on the right, both words must be on the same slip.

example: **company Angestellte**

Mix up the slips and ask your fellow students to stand in a circle in groups of three or four with each person holding one of the slips. Make sure that each slip translates correctly both to the left and to the right.

example: **cwo Gesellschaft** ↔ **company Angestellte** ↔ **employee Lieferant**

It does not matter which slip you begin with, if you lay the slips correctly you will form a circle.

to avoid Lumpen	rags Gehalt	salary Vertreter
representative Prozess	process Faß	barrel Betrag
amount oben	above LKW	lorry brutto
gross Verlust	loss messen	to measure beurteilen
to judge Eigentum	property Meinung	opinion höflich
polite Schüler	pupil Hafen	harbour Rechnung
invoice Rollgeld	cartage Größe	size Antwort
reply/answer dienen	to serve Grafschaft	county Zellulose
cellulose Spalte	column Prozentsatz	percentage Messe
fair auffallend	eye-catching Staub	dust Prüfung

COPY

By Appointment to
HM the Queen
Paper Merchants

MoDo

MoDo
Office Service Ltd
Office Papers

Rosemount Avenue
West Byfleet
SURREY KT14 6LE
Tel 0932 335577
Fax 0932 335580

Purchase Stock Card

SUPPLIERS:

1 No.

Name:

Address:

Telephone:

Fax:

Discount:

Terms of delivery:

Time of delivery:

Terms of payment:

2 No.

Name:

Address:

Telephone:

Fax:

Discount:

Terms of delivery:

Time of delivery:

Terms of payment:

Minimum stock quantity:	Article number:
Notify quantity:	Article name:
Maximum stock:	Unit:

Supplier No.	date		order		acknow.* of order	invoice		amount		list price per unit		payment date
	enquiry	offer	date	quantity	date	No.	date	£	p	£	p	

* acknowledgement of order

Purchase Movements Card

Article name:	Article No.:	Unit:

Minimum quantity:	Notify quantity:	Maximum quantity:

Supplier No.:	Supplier No.:
Name:	Name:
Address:	Address:

Notification of requirements (warehouse department and dispatch)					Order placed by the purchasing department						reminder
date	quantity in stock	quantity needed	date of delivery	signature	date			quantity ordered	supplier No.	approx. date of delivery	
					enquiry	offer	order				

Warehouse Stock Card

Article No.:		Article name:				Unit:	
Minimum stock:			Order stock:		Maximum stock:		
Stock movement					Restock order		
date	document No.	receipt	exit	in stock	date	order quantity	signature